Blueprint For Localism
A Different Kind of Greenhouse

John L. Robitaille

Copyright © 2024 Robitaille John Larkin

All Rights Reserved

Dedication

I wish to dedicate this book to my wife, Jan, who has offered encouragement and guidance.

Acknowledgment

My appreciation to all those who have shown a genuine interest in the nature of this subject. Their enthusiasm has been a big boost in completing this book.

CONTENTS

Dedication iii

Acknowledgment iv

List of Illustrations vii

Table of Parts List x

About The Author xii

Preface xiii

Chapter 1 1

   1.   Environmental Challenge 1

      1.1 LED Lighting 1

      1.2 Environmental Control 2

      1.3 Vertical Farming 2

   2.   Description of the Greenhouse 7

      2.1 Cement Column Installation 7

      2.2 Base Wall Construction 13

      2.3 North and South Wall Construction 20

      2.4 Rafter Sizing and Installation 24

      2.5 East and West Wall Studs 31

      2.6 East and West Wall Siding 36

2.7 Roofing 42

2.8 Insulation 46

2.9 Ventilator - Air Conditioner and Retractable Cover ... 47

2.10 Shelving 51

2.11 Plumbing 56

2.12 Wiring 62

2.13 LED Lighting and Timers 71

2.14 Shelf Design and Fabrication 73

2.15 Preparation and Cleaning Counter 76

Summary 79

Bibliography 80

Notes 82

List of Illustrations

Figure 2.1-1 .... Locating Columns

Figure 2.1-2...................... Installing Cement Columns

Figure 2.2-1...................... Base Wall Fabrication

Figure 2.2-2 .... Polyethylene Liner, Sand, and Topsoil

Figure 2.2-3 .... Radiant Heating Tubing Layout

Figure 2.3-1 .... North and South Wall Construction

Figure 2.3-2......................Siding, Painting North and South Walls

Figure 2.4-1 .... Ridge Board Support Column

Figure 2.4-2 .... North Rafter Size

Figure 2.4-3...................... South Rafter Size

Figure 2.4-4 .... Rafter Cross Ties for Polycarbonate

Figure 2.5-1 .... Miter Blocks for Studs

Figure 2.5-2 .... West Side Stud Sizes

Figure 2.5-3 .... East Side Stud Sizes

Figure 2.6-1 .... Siding West Side - Lower

Figure 2.6-2..................... Siding West Side – Upper

Figure 2.6-3 .... Siding East Side - Lower

Figure 2.6-4..................... Siding East Side – Upper

Figure 2-7-1..................... Sheathing, Underlayment, Metal Roof - North

Figure 2-7-2..................... Sheathing, Underlayment, Metal Roof – South

Figure 2.7-3 ....Roof PolyCarbonate Panels Install

Figure 2.8-1..................... Interior Insulation

Figure 2.9-1..................... Ventilator Installation

Figure 2.9-2..................... Air Conditioner Installation

Figure 2.9-3..................... Retractable Cover Deployed

Figure 2.10-1................... Horizontal Rail Support Sub-Assembly

Figure 2-10-2................... Column Support for Shelves

Figure 2.10-3................... LED Support Boards

Figure 2.11-1 .... Plumbing Schematic

Figure 2.11-2…………………...Water Tank/Circulating Pump Installation

Figure 2.12-1………………… Wiring – Overall View

Figure 2.12-2……………….. Wiring – Main Panel Circuits

Figure 2.12-3……………….. Wiring – LED Outlets and Timers

Figure 2.12-4 ………………. Wiring - Overhead Lighting

Figure 2.12-5…………………...Wiring–Thermal Switch Air Conditioner/Ventilator

Figure 2.12-6 ………………. Wiring – Thermal Switch Raised Bed

Figure 2.13-1……………….. LED Installation

Figure 2.14-1……………….. Shelf Design

Figure 2.14-2……………….. Shelf Bearing Installation

Figure 2.15-1……………….. Preparation and Cleaning Counter

Table of Parts List

Table 2.1 .... Cement Column Parts List

Table 2.2 .... Base Wall Parts List

Table 2.3 .... North South Wall Construction Parts List

Table 2.4 .... Rafter Sizing Parts List

Table 2.5 .... East and West Wall Studs Parts List

Table 2.6 .... East and West Wall Siding Parts List

Table 2.7 .... Roofing Parts List

Table 2.8.... Insulation Parts List

Table 2.9 .... Ventilator, Air Conditioner and Retractable Cover Parts List

Table 2.10 ...Shelving Supports Parts List

Table 2.11 ...Plumbing Parts List

Table 2.12 ...Wiring Parts List

Table 2.13 ...LED Lighting and Timers Parts List

Table 2.14... Shelf Fabrication Parts List

Table 2.15 ... Preparation and Cleaning Counter Parts List

Page Blank Intentionally

About The Author

John Robitaille is a retired Aerospace Engineer that saw this book as an opportunity to present part of a solution to Climate Change as well as rising food prices. He has built two houses and wanted to share some approaches to constructing this greenhouse. In his spare time John enjoys skiing, rowing, swimming, and cycling.

Preface

Having worked in Michigan for a decade plus, instead of flying, I had to drive my car back to Connecticut for an auto emissions test. The route was simple: head to Ohio and then follow Interstate 80 straight shot across Ohio, Pennsylvania, New York and into Connecticut. I had never driven 12 hours in one day and never got to see much of this part of the country. One thing that was not apparent when flying was the intensity of tractor-trailer traffic. There were lots of them – the usual one-box, but plenty of 2 boxes and an occasional three-box trailers being hauled by those big semis that have bulldogs as a hood ornament.

Much of this traffic was merchandise headed to the likes of Walmart and Costco of the world, but many contained raw produce. This is easy to spot by noticing the number of reefers – slang for refrigerated trailers that stand out. They have refrigeration boxes attached to the rear of each cab or on the front of the trailer. After some additional web surfing, I discovered that 90% of our food is transported to market via reefers.[1] At the time of this writing, an average reefer costs $2.37 per mile. That is understandable when the average semi only gets about 6 MPG.

There is extensive data collected by the United States Department of Agriculture [3] on the costs for transporting refrigerated food for the short, and long hauls. After a review of this data, that alone was an additional incentive in writing this book about providing not only fresh, and in some cases, organic food locally but also significantly reducing Green House Gases – (GHGs).

For produce leaving California and destined for Boston, New York, and Philadelphia – the cost of transport alone per trailer can easily exceed $7,000. A study [2] conducted at Stanford University highlights some of these statistics, plus the spoilage and subsequent waste of food when being transported over long distances. Also, additional energy is expended to plant, irrigate, harvest, package and warehouse these crops.

Chapter 1

1. Environmental Challenge

The idea for this book was more than just an unforeseen wake-up call to wasted energy; it was a merger of how resources such as water, soil and a massive transportation network are taken for granted. Many rural areas lack access to grocery stores, which in turn requires, in some cases, traveling long distances to get food. With a greenhouse, one has control over what goes into the soil along with what goes on in the plants during the growth cycle. This leaves plenty of room for improvement. At this moment, I realized that here has got to be a better way. What would it take to make a greenhouse that could produce four yields in a year? So, I set out to design a greenhouse, complete with radiant heating, LED lighting and vertical farming. The number of sunny days per year for many is also limited, and using a greenhouse is restricted due to neighboring trees and buildings. This design overcomes that, with the only requirement being access to electricity. I go through the sequences of constructing each part. To help accelerate the process for those wishing to do the same.

I provide a parts list at the end of each section of the key components.

1.1 LED Lighting

LED lighting is a low-cost method of providing artificial light to the plants. Regardless of the amount of sunshine, latitude, or time of year, the plants can be assured of the proper amount of light. It is cheaper to operate than fluorescent lights, and they last much longer.

LED emits specific colors that are conducive to promoting plant growth both when they are seedlings and when maturing. These are used in concert with timers, which can provide just the right amount of lighting required.

1.2 Environmental Control

Warm temperatures at the roots of the plant benefit the rate of plant growth. One of the key features of this greenhouse is the use of radiant heat by implementing a warm water loop of plumbing embedded in the soil. This not only accelerates plant growth but also warms the interior of the greenhouse. For the best vegetable germination and growth rate, the soil temperature should be warmer than 70 Degrees Fahrenheit [4]. See Table I.

The heated water that is circulated is maintained by means of an electric hot water tank. It is safe, has a low initial cost, does not emit toxic gases and requires no labor for sustaining heat. However, electricity rates vary amongst states [5], so this could be a determinant factor in using electricity to heat as well as illuminate a garden with LED lighting. Table II lists by state the average price of electricity per kilowatt-hour. And for those warm days, ventilation is crucial since overheating of the plants can ruin a whole cycle of plantings. Therefore, accommodations for either a temperature-activated ventilator or air conditioner are included in this design.

1.3 Vertical Farming

Vertical farming has recently experienced rapid growth. Vertical farms are being located adjacent to large cities and, in so doing, have become a source of fresh produce for selective restaurants and grocers. This design incorporates vertical farming as a way to move seedlings to their next stage selectively and to remove those that have not germinated. The investment and construction of a firm wooden structure make this possible.

Table I – Ideal Germination Temperatures

Crop	Germination Minimum Soil Temperature (°F)	Germination Optimum Soil Temperature Range (°F)	Germination Maximum Soil Temperature (°F)	Days to Germination at Optimal Temps
Asparagus	50	60-85	95	14-18
Bean, lima	60	75-85	85	4-10
Bean, snap	60	75-85	95	4-10
Beet	40	60-85	95	4-10
Broccoli	40	60-85	95	7-10
Brussels sprouts	40	60-85	95	3-10
Carrot	40	65-85	95	6
Cauliflower	40	65-85	95	4-10
Celery	40	60-70	95	10
Chinese Cabbage	40	60-85	95	4-10
Collards	40	60-85	95	5-10
Corn	50	65-95	105	5-10
Cucumber	60	65-95	105	5-7
Eggplant	60	75-85	95	10-15
Endive/Escarole	35	60-75	85	10-14
Garlic	35	65-85	95	7-14
Kale	40	60-85	95	5-7

Kohlrabi	40	60-95	105	5-19
Leeks	35	65-85	95	8-16
Lettuce	35	60-75	85	2-10
Muskmelon	60	75-95	105	4-10
Mustard	35	60-75	85	4-6
Okra	60	85-95	105	7-12
Onion	35	65-85	95	4-12
Parsley	40	65-85	95	5-6 weeks
Parsnip	35	65-75	85	5-28
Pea	40	65-75	85	5-7
Pepper	60	65-75	95	7=10
Pumpkin	60	85-95	105	4-10
Radicchio	35	60-75	85	5-7
Radish	40	65-85	95	4-10
Spinach	35	65-75	75	7-10
Squash	60	85-95	105	7-10
Swiss Chard	40	65-85	95	7-10
Tomato	50	65-85	95	5-7
Turnip	40	60-95	105	3-10
Watermelon	60	70-95	105	4-10

Table II - Cost of Electricity per Kw-Hr (Jan. 2019)

State	$/Kw-hr	State	$/Kw-hr	State	$/Kw-hr
AK	.218	KY	.103	NY	.173
AL	.117	LA	.091	OH	.122
AR	.093	MA	.22	OK	.089
AZ	.1212	MD	.131	OR	.107
CA	.183	ME	.173	PA	.126
CO	.119	MI	.150	RI	.227
CT	.215	MN	.125	SC	.121
DC	.130	MO	.096	SD	.106
DE	.121	MS	.109	TN	.109
FL	.1165	MT	.106	TX	.114
GA	.110	NC	.109	UT	.099
HI	.321	ND	.091	VA	.115
IA	.105	NE	.095	VT	.168
ID	.098	NH	.20	WA	.094
IL	.124	NJ	.157	WI	.135
IN	.121	NM	.122	WV	.098
KS	.103	NV	.118	WY	.105

2. Description of the Greenhouse

This book addresses the basic design features required to construct a beneficial environment for growing vegetables all year long. My objective is to make it a low-cost, simple, yet durable structure that maximizes the number of plants for a given footprint. This greenhouse is unique in that it uses radiant heating in the raised beds, while the structural design facilitates vertical farming. Vertical farming is growing in popularity simply because there is less land area required. This generates more produce close to urban centers. It is being deployed increasingly in abandoned factory buildings, especially in Europe. Ideally, for some crops, it can produce up to 4 yields per year. A parts list table is included in each section, which expedites the construction process.

2.1 Cement Column Installation

The corners of the greenhouse are established by driving eight rebar (3 feet long) stakes at the locations shown in Figure 2.1-1. The distances between the lengths and widths need to be established (16 feet x 20 feet) and the diagonals confirmed. A taut nylon string is connected to each corner, and the string must be kept in the same plane as the others by using a line level. Sonotubes function as cement forms.

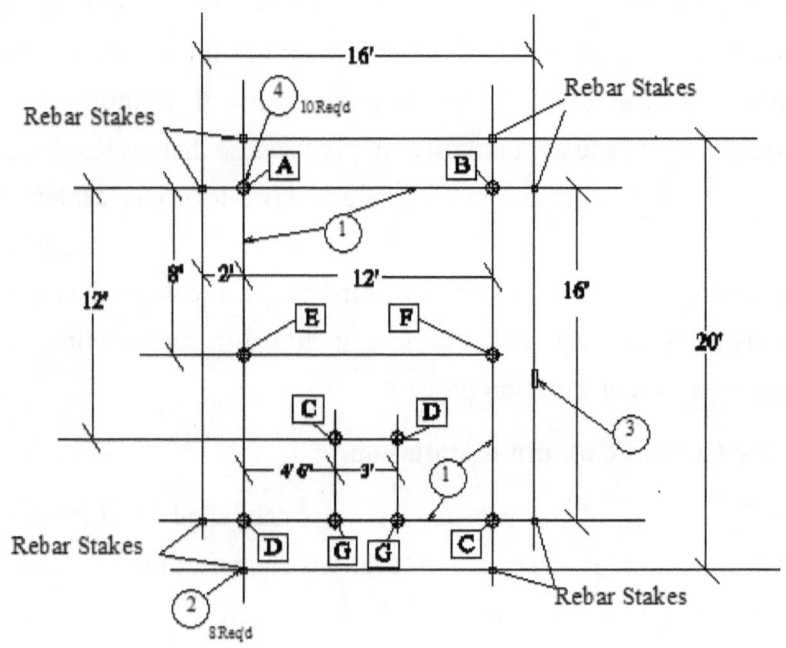

Figure 2.1-1 - Locating Columns

With these strings in place, proceed to excavate the four corner locations for sonotube forms. Six additional sonotubes are required one each for the mid-span of the sixteen-foot wall, one on each side to form the inside opening for the doorway entrance and one each to support the interior corner of the Base Wall. For this design, the doorway width is 34 inches.

At each of the ten sonotube locations, holes approximately eight inches in diameter and 2 feet deep will need to be dug. Eight-inch diameter augers can be rented or bought. See Figure 2.1-2.

The appropriate orientation of the brackets and their type is shown in Figure 2.1-3.

When the brackets are placed on the top of the concrete columns, ¼ inch x 3-inch threaded studs are inserted through the holes in the brackets and pressed into the cement, allowing at least one inch of thread to protrude above the bracket once the cement has cured, secure the brackets to the sonotubes with ¼ inch nuts and washers. Two studs, nuts, and washers per configurations shown in A, B, C (2) and D (2) with 2 each for a total of 12. Three are required per configurations shown in E, F and G (2) with 3 each for a total of 12.

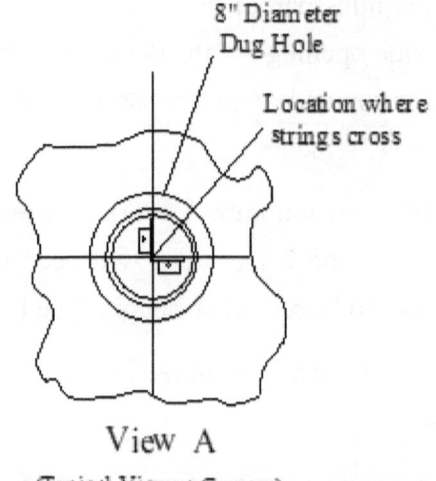

View A
(Typical View at Corners)

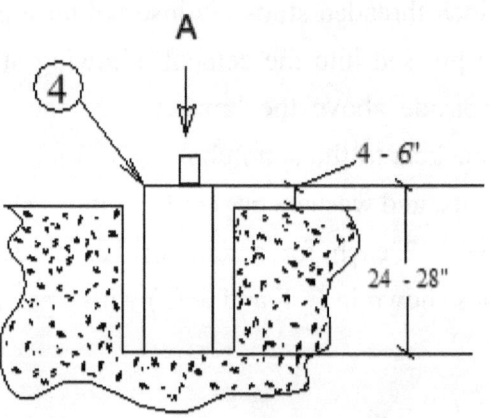

Figure 2.1-2 - Installing Cement Columns

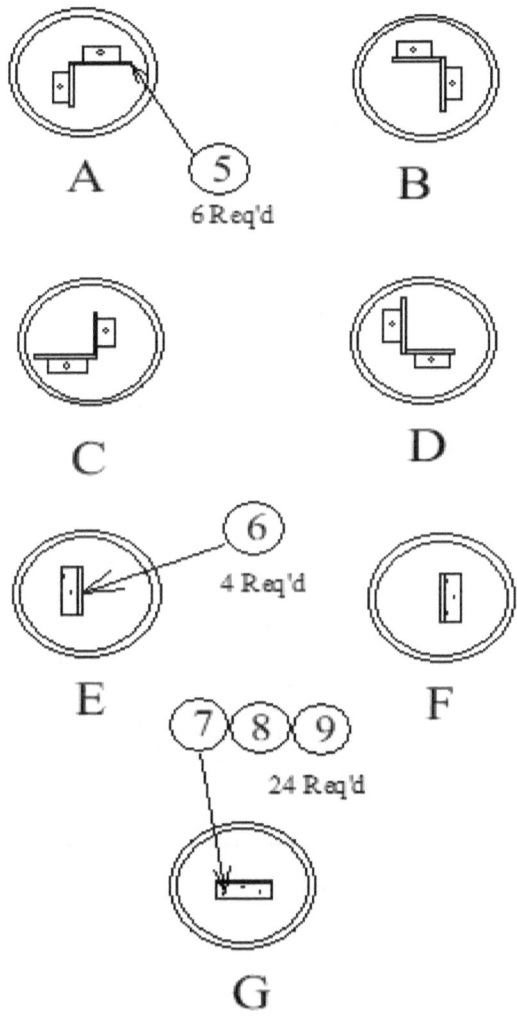

Figure 2.1-3 - Base Bracket Install

Table 2.1 Cement Column Parts List

Item	Qty	Description	Source	SKU
1	1	Orange Nylon String – 250 ft.	Home Depot	1002277397
2	2	0.5"X 10' Black Steel Rebar	Lowes	12166
3	1	Aluminum Line Level	Home Depot	157438
4	10	Sonotubes – 8" x 48"	Home Depot	285266
5	6	Tie Common – 2" x 4"	Lowes	1944524
6	4	Tie 2"x2"x4" Galv. Steel Angle	Lowes	312975
7	24	0.25"x3" (SAE) Threaded Rod	Lowes	137923
8	24	¼"x 20 Zn-Plated Steel Hex Nut	Lowes	63301
9	24	¼" Standard Flat Washer	Lowes	58124

2.2 Base Wall Construction

The Base Wall consists of an exterior perimeter and two separate interior sections that form the boundaries for the raised beds. Each of these Base Wall sections consists of two horizontally stacked 2" x 10" boards that are kept in place by 2" x 4"s vertical supports that are screwed to both the lower and upper 2" x 10" boards.

For the interior boards that make up the enclosed bed, their respective corners each rest on cement-filled sonotubes, while the ends of the lower Base Walls that are perpendicular to other Base walls are suspended by floor joist brackets. These brackets are secured to the lower Base Wallboards. The door opening for the east-end wall will be determined by the size of the door used. For this design, a 34-inch-wide Dutch-style door is used. This allows for plenty of room to get materials and produce into and out of the greenhouse. The base wall widths for each side are calculated by subtracting the width of the door frame from 12 feet and dividing by two and then adding 3 inches for trim. For this door, the width will be (12 x 12" -34 -3)/2 = 53.5 inches. Proceed to cut the four baseboards (2" x 10") to this length and then secure them so it is flush to the interior edge on each side of the door frame and with the other end secured to the outer edge of the sideboards. The opening height, as determined from the top of the cement sonotubes is 6'10". Enough clearance is allowed for the door and installation of ¾" finish trim. Once the Base Walls have been constructed, the interior wall needs to be covered with a rigid Foam Board to assist in retaining the Raised Bed heat. Also, the retention of moisture and sustaining a warm subsoil is enhanced by attaching two layers of 6-mil polyethylene to the interior base walls of the garden bed. This can be done simply by nailing thin ¼" x 1-1/2" lath strips along the upper edge of the inner perimeter of the garden beds. Allow the polyethylene to be very loose in adapting to the bottom contour of the garden bed.

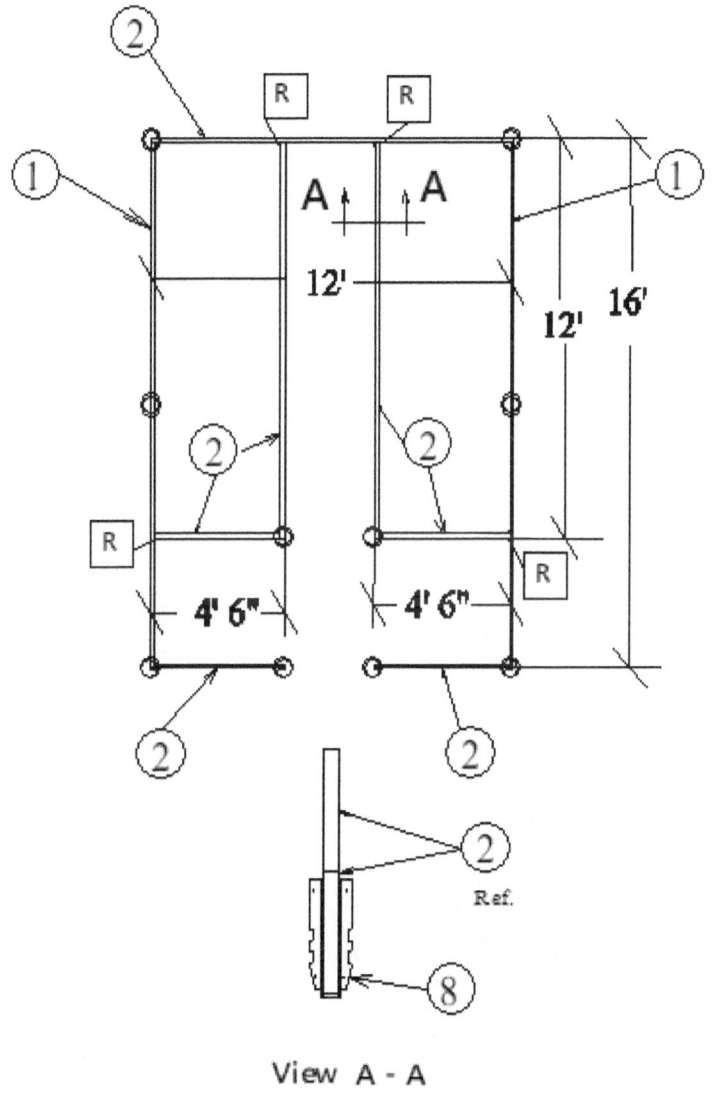

Figure 2.2-1 - Base Wall Fabrication

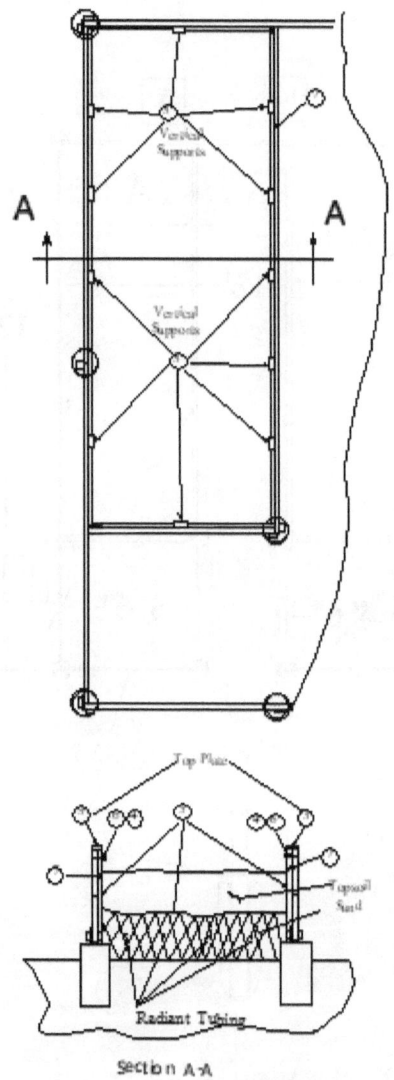

Figure 2.2-2 - Polyethylene Liner, Sand, and Topsoil

For those who may have a concern about plant contamination from the chemicals used in pressure-treated lumber (primarily arsenic in CCA – Chromated Copper Arsenate), there should not be a problem. [6] The sale of CCA-treated lumber was restricted by the EPA in 2004. To be on the safe side, use polyethylene.

Heat distribution to the roots of the plants is accomplished by circulating warm water through ½" PEX tubing installed within the sand layer. This will require drilling ¾" holes at two locations on each of the garden beds. These holes will provide an entrance and exit for the PEX tubing on each of the garden beds. The first entrance will be on the right garden bed at 2 inches above the bottom edge of the lower baseboard. The minimum bend radius for ½" PEX tubing is 5 inches, so to achieve this coverage, the first layer should be placed at 12-inch intervals to preclude the kinking of the tubing.

Even distribution of the heat from the radiant tubing is best done with sand. An additional layer of six inches of sand will be applied to cover the PEX tubing. This will ensure a large reservoir of heat storage created by the warm water circulating through the PEX tubing while also offering a means where the heat can be slowly dissipated evenly to the plants. A top layer of at least 3 inches of compost followed by 6 to 10 inches of topsoil should be added to the top of the sand.

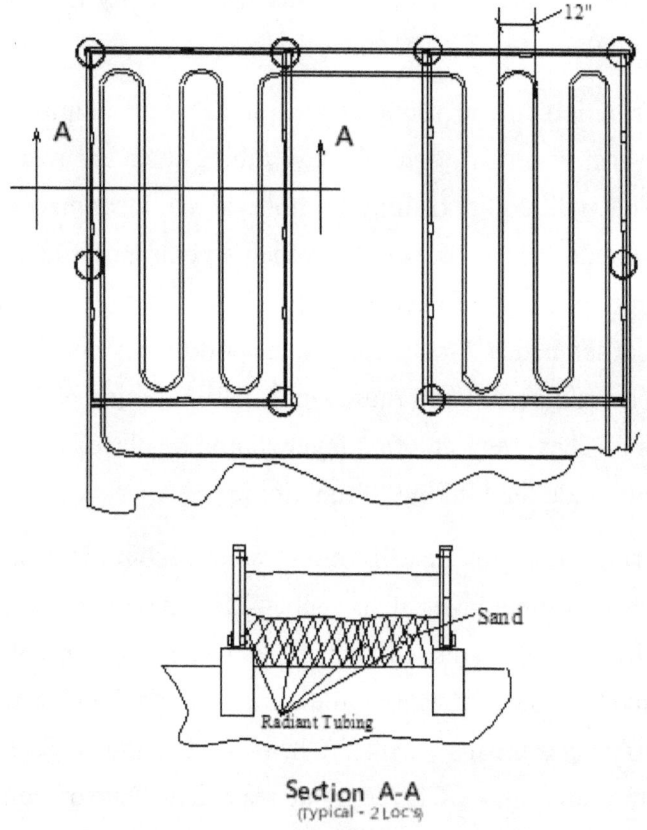

Figure 2.2-3 Radiant Heating - Tubing Layout

Table 2.2 Base Wall Parts List

Item	Qty	Description	Source	SKU
1	8	2" x 10" x 16' Press Treated	Home Depot	1001787117
2	6	2" x 10" x 12' Press Treated	Home Depot	1001787116
3	AR	2" x 4" x 8' Press Treated	Home Depot	1001787122
4	AR	3" Squeek Screws	Home Depot	1000863053
5	1	Polyethylene – 6 mill thickness	Home Depot	756377
6	AR	¼" x 1-1/2" x 6' Press Treated Lath	Home Depot	1001311054
7	6	FOAMULAR F-150 1"x4'x8'Rigid Foam Board	Home Depot	------------
8	4	Hanger 2" x 10"	Lowes	108802
9	AR	Strong-Tie #9 x 1-1/2-in Wood Screws	Lowes	130014

2.3 North and South Wall Construction

The north and south wall partitions are two separate walls that are constructed in order to support the greenhouse rafters. To ensure a stable footing for these partitions, a layer of 2" x 4" base plates needs to be secured to the top of the base wall. Additional stability is rendered by securing 2" x 4" boards along the upper inside edge of the upper base walls. With the base plate in place, proceed to construct the two 16-foot-long partitions with a height, as shown in Figure 2.3-1. To maintain plumb positions for the partitions, secure two braces each between the top edge of the partition and the top edge of the garden bed base wall.

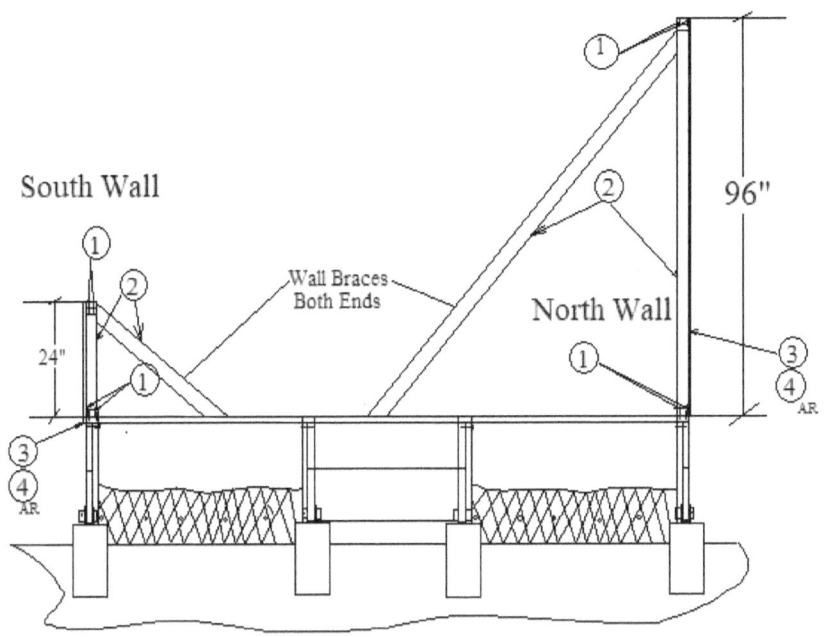

Figure 2.3-1 North and South Wall Construction

Since the overall dimensions for rafter sizing include the additional width of the siding, its installation on the North and South side walls needs to be done next. The preferred siding is cedar panels, which are 3/8" thick. Starting with the north side, cut the siding to length and install with stainless steel nails.

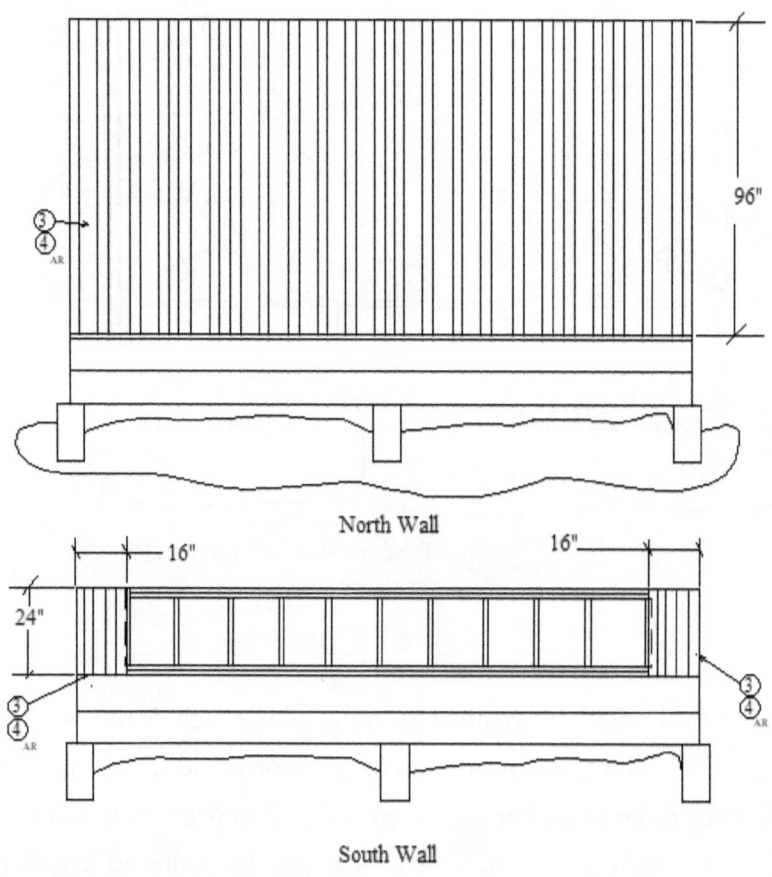

Figure 2.3-2 Siding and Painting North and South Walls

Table 2.3 North South Wall Construction Parts List

Item	Qty	Description	Source	SKU
1	1	3" Squeek Screws	Home Depot	1000863053
2	AR	2" x 4" x 8'	Home Depot	161640
3	5	Cedar Texture Siding 4'x8' x .35"	Home Depot	509095
4	AR	Stainless Ribbed Nails 2" – 13 Ga	Lowes	41976

2.4 Rafter Sizing and Installation

A ridge board support column will need to be erected at each end of the East and West Base Walls. This support column assembly will temporarily hold the ridge board in place until the rafters are tied into the ridge board. The main column is cut to the length as shown in Figure 2.4-1. The ridge board is held in place laterally by two side blocks that are screwed to the support column at the top. To ensure the assembly is plumb, a Column Base Bracket is pre-fabricated and installed. Then, install the column support at a 90-degree angle and fasten it to the Column Base Bracket.

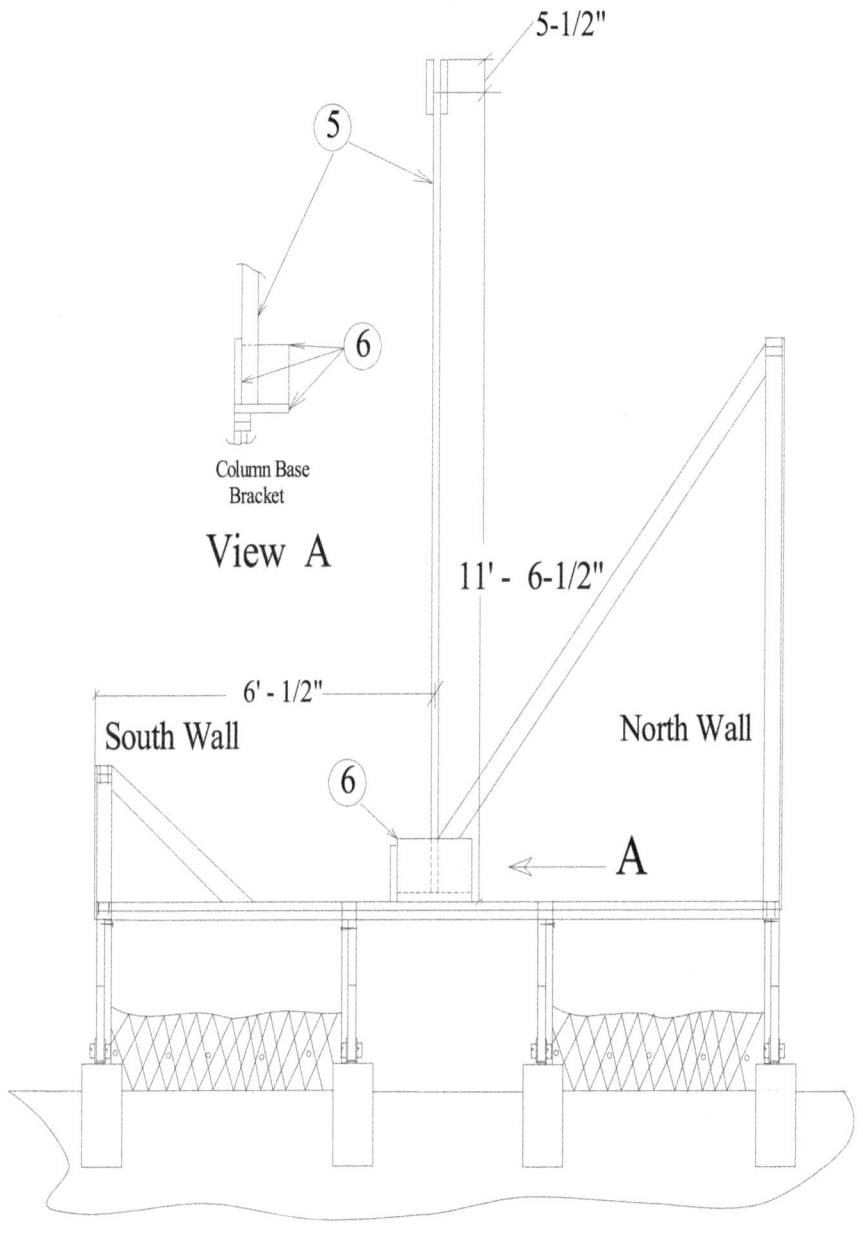

Figure 2.4-1 Ridge Board Support Columns

25

The North rafter is cut from an 8 foot 2" x 6" board. Measure off the top length of the rafter as shown in Figure 2.4-2. With the two markings established, use a rafter square and draw the two respective angles as illustrated for the two ends. Reference backup dimensions are shown to confirm the correct angles. However, for the lower end of the rafter, a "bird's mouth" or stop in the rafter is made so it will engage with the North Wall partition firmly. Two small additional cuts are made to accommodate the placement of small soffit and fascia boards.

The South rafter is cut from a 12 foot 2" x 6" board. Repeat the same procedure as outlined for the North rafter but per the dimensions as shown in Figure 2.4-3. For backup, reference dimensions to the angular settings are shown in Figure 2.4-3. Also, make the necessary cuts to accommodate the fascia and soffit boards.

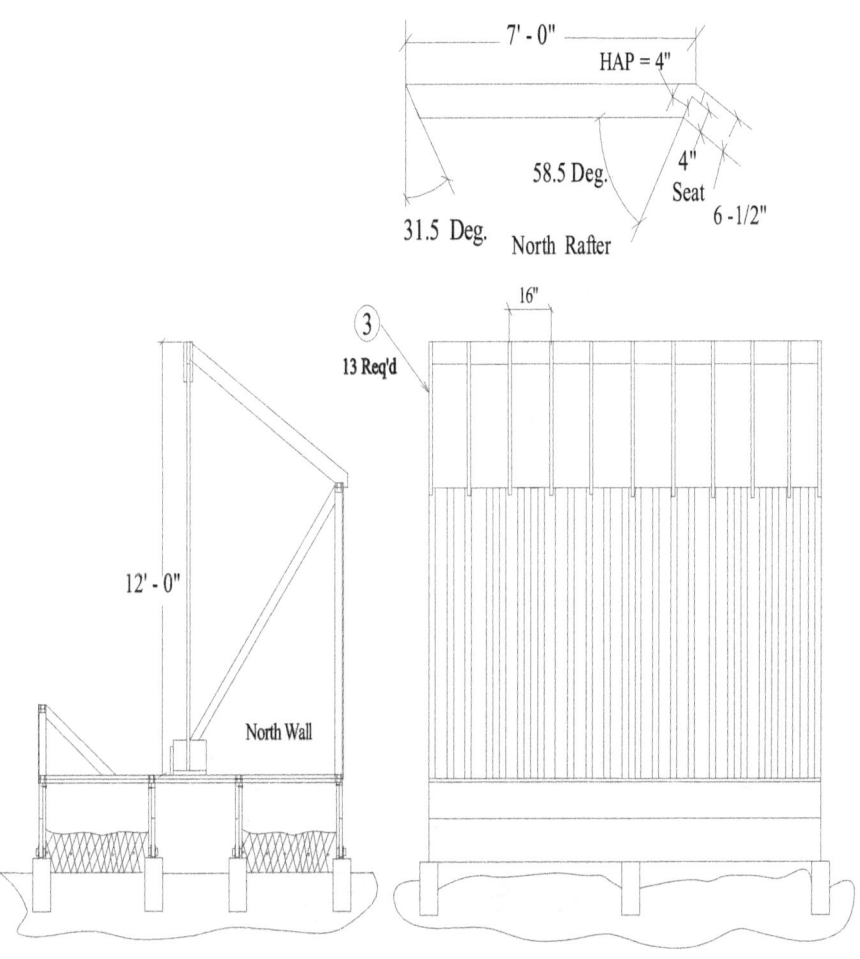

Figure 2.4-2 North Rafter Size

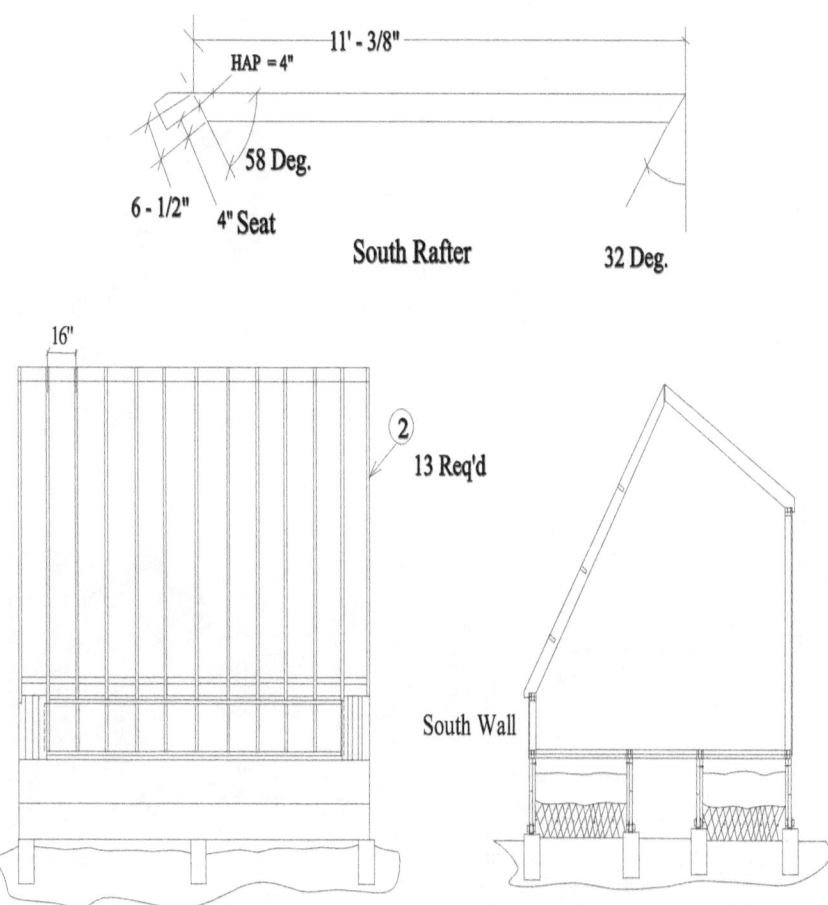

Figure 2.4-3 South Rafter Size

Once the ridge rafter is put into place, it must be maintained in a straight line from one end to the other. Drive one nail at the top of each end of the ridge rafter and then secure a taunt line of string between each end. When installing the rafters, use the string as a guide for straightness. Then, starting at one end, mark off 16-inch increments in the center along the ridge rafter as well as along the north and south walls. Since the ridge rafter support columns exist at each end, forego installing the first and last rafters. They can be installed once the others are in place.

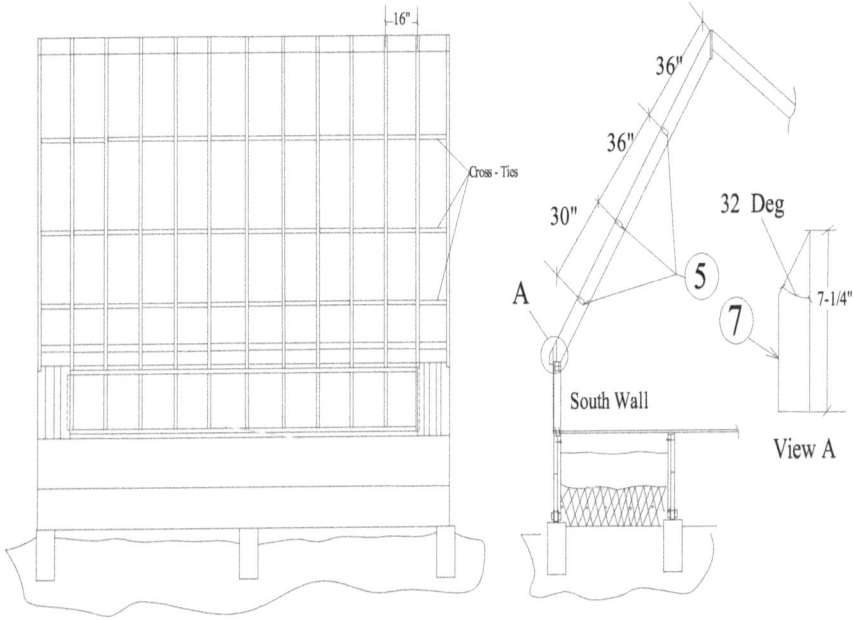

Figure 2.4-4 Rafter Installation and Cross Ties for Polycarbonate Panels

Being that a good portion of the south rafters will be covered with polycarbonate panels, lateral support will be required to preclude sagging under a snow load. Therefore, since the rafters are spaced at 16 inches, the cross members will be 14-1/2" in length and made up of 2" x 4"s. They should be placed 24" apart along the length of the rafters.

Table 2.4 Rafter Sizing Parts List

Item	Qty	Description	Source	SKU
1	1	2" x 6" x16'	Lowes	432483
2	13	2" x 6" x12'	Lowes	432486
3	13	2" x 6" x 8'	Lowes	432484
4	AR	3" Squeek Screws	Home Depot	1000863053
5	5	2" x 4" x 12'	Lowes	196496
6	1	2" x 12" x 8'	Lowes	WF212TOPCHC08
7	2	2" x 8" x 8'	Lowes	278248

2.5 East and West Wall Studs

The end walls are made up of 2" x 4" studs that are used to support the west exterior wall, which consists of Cedar Siding Panels. Since the angle of the south rafters is so steep and beyond the settings and depths of most table and circular saws, making custom miter blocks may be required.

The angle for both the north and south rafters is 58 degrees. Using a rafter/speed square, mark off the 58-degree angle on three 2" x 4" blocks. Once layered and secured together, the three mitered blocks will have a minimum height of 4 -1/2", which is sufficiently high enough to support a 2" x 4" board when positioned on the edge. This way, the angled end of the stud will match the angle of the respective rafters. See Figure 2.5-1.

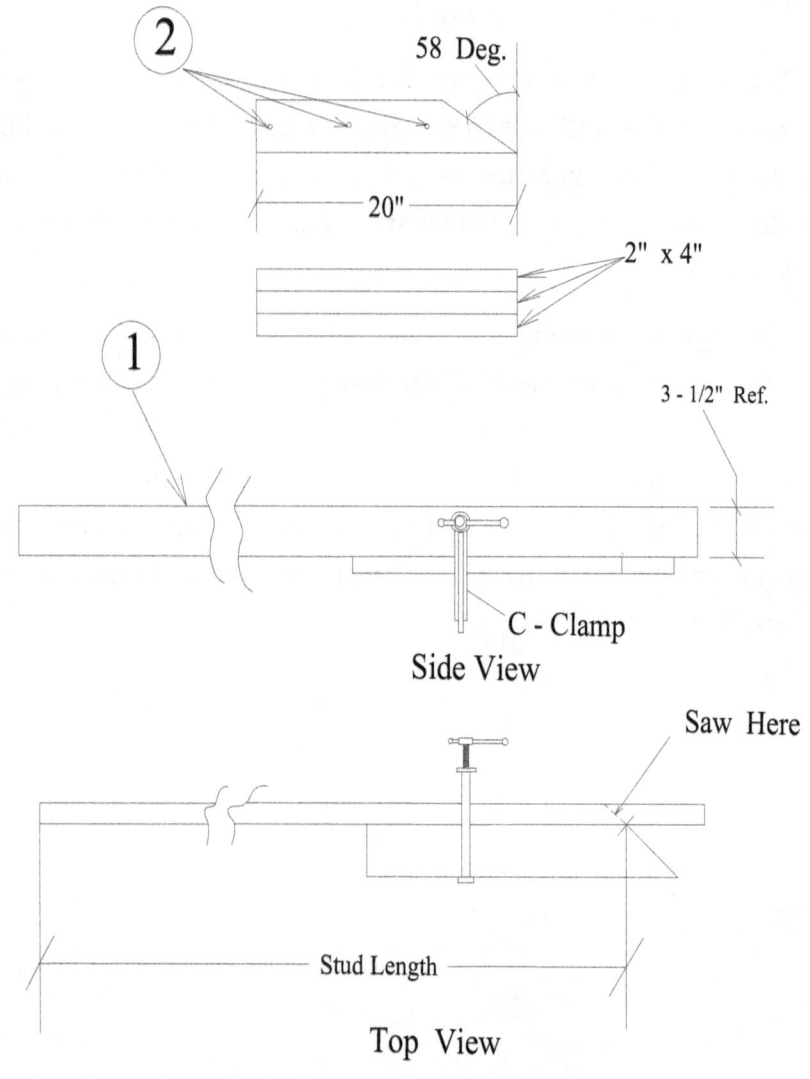

Figure 2.5-1 Miter Block Fabrication
and in Use

Space each 2" x 4" at 16" on center by using a small 2" x 4" block fastened besides the stud into the base plate. Using a level, ensure each stud is plumb or at 90 degrees to the base plate, and with a pencil, mark a line on the stud where it intersects with the end rafter. For these studs at 58 degrees, the three-miter block assembly is to be cut at the proper angle. Studs cut at 32 degrees can be done with a circular saw. See Table 2.5-1 for the West Side angles and Figure 2.5-2. Studs cut at 32 degrees can be done with a circular saw or table saw. Repeat the same procedure for the East Side per Table 2.5-2 and Figure 2.5-3.

Table 2.5-1 West Wall Stud Lengths and Angles

Stud Number	Angle
1	58
2	58
3	58
4	58
5	32
6	32
7	32
8	32

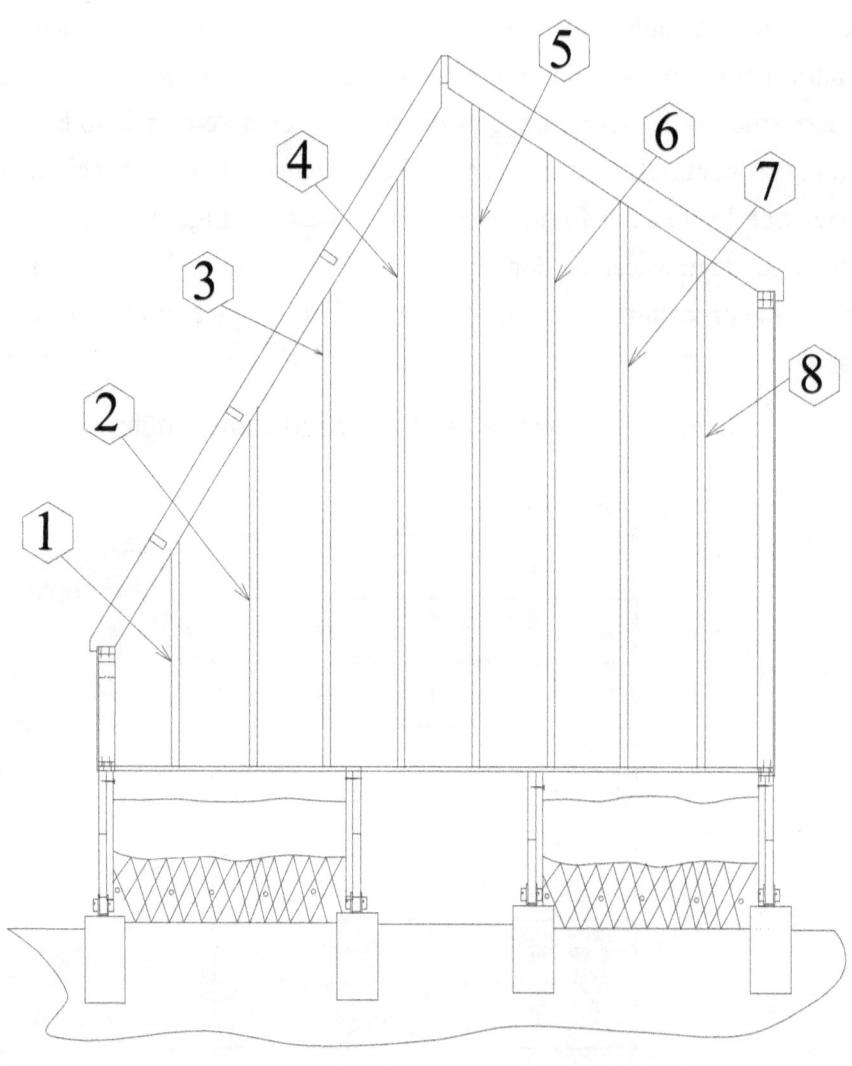

Figure 2.5-2 West Side Stud Sizes

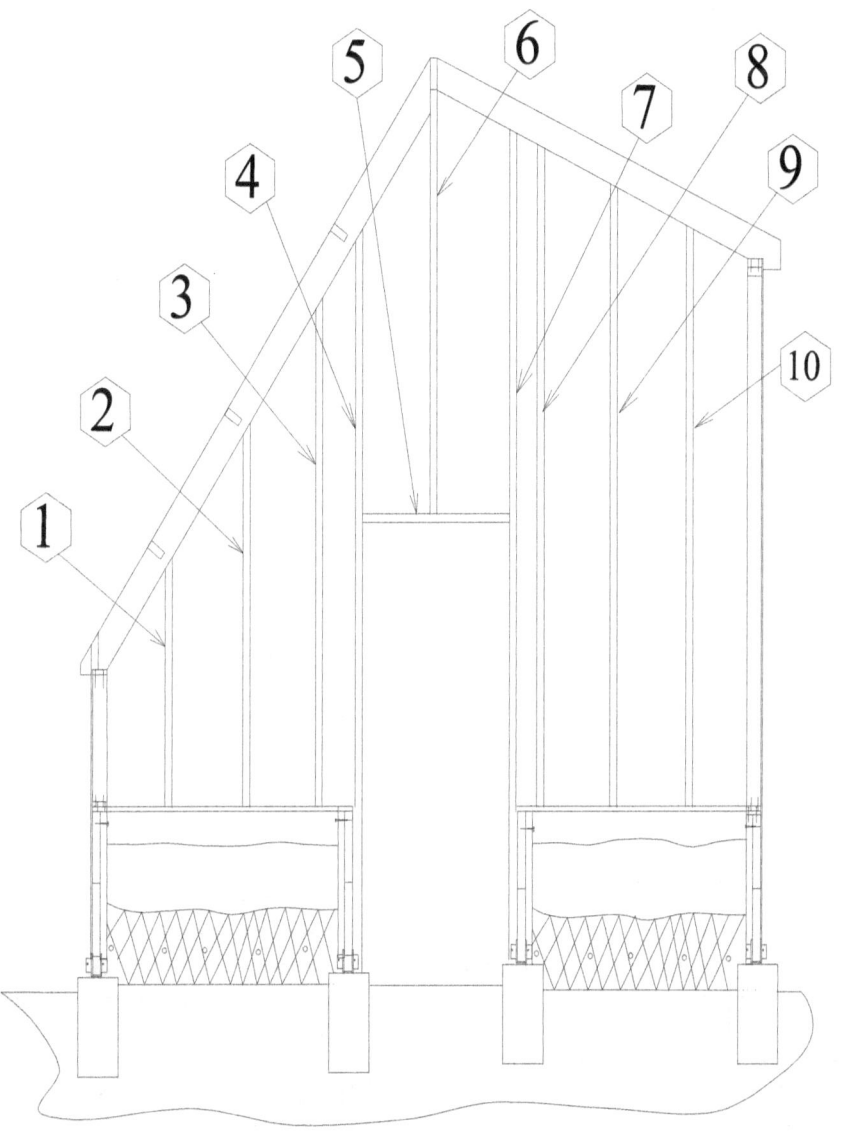

Figure 2.5-3 East Side Stud Sizes

Table 2.5-2 East Wall Stud Lengths and Angles

Stud Number	Angle
1	58
2	58
3	58
4	58
5	0
6	0
7	32
8	32
9	32
10	32

Table 2.5-3 East and West Wall Studs Parts List

Item	Qty	Description	Source	SKU
1	AR	2" x4" x 8'	Home Depot	161640
2	AR	3" Squeek Screws	Home Depot	1000863053

2.6 East and West Wall Siding

Secure a 2" x 4" cleat along the top edge of the upper 2" x 10" Base Board. Starting at the North side rest 2 Panels on the cleat and secure to the studs on the West Side. For the third panel, position its lower edge on top of the cleat and temporarily secure the Cedar Panel with two screws - one at the top and one at the bottom. Once in place, using the top surface of the rafter as an edge, trace with a pencil where the Cedar Panel extends above the rafter. Remove the Cedar Panel and cut along the penciled line. Then fasten the Texture 1-11 panel to the 2 x 4 studs. Once the three Panels are in place, cut to length the Z-flashing drip edge along the top edge of the Panels. Nail the flashing to the studs. The Upper Panels can then be sized by using a tape measure and then cutting the length and height measurements for each. The length of the panel may need to be shortened so it aligns with a stud. See Figure 2.6-1.

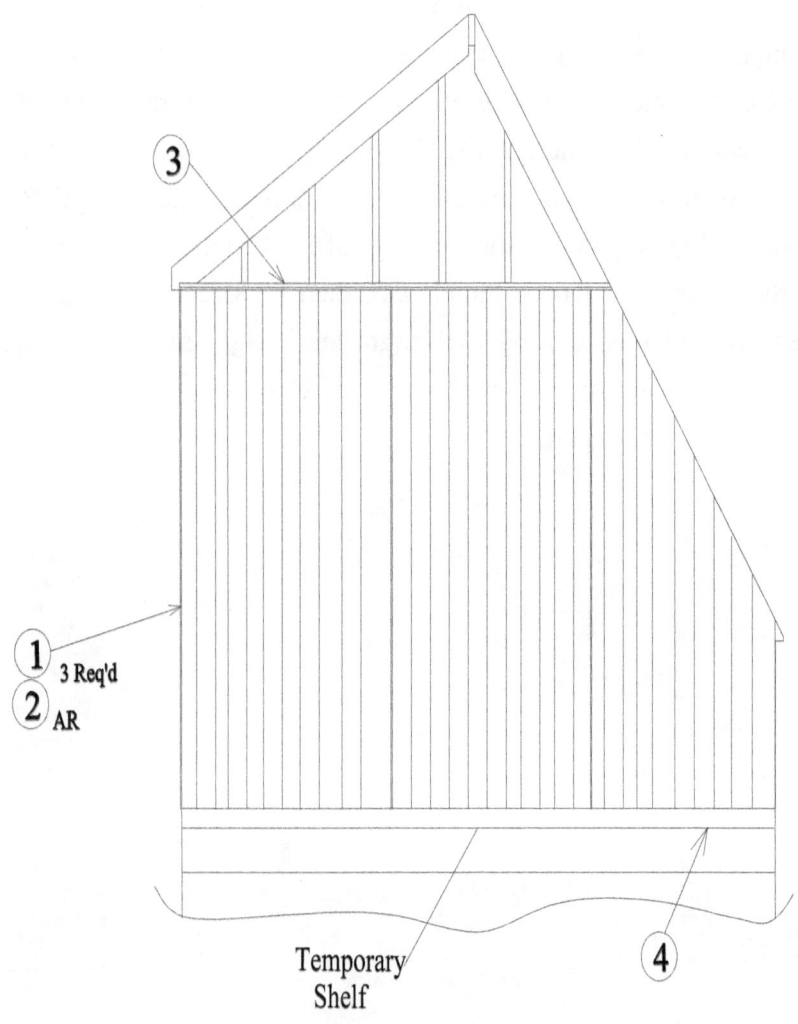

Figure 2.6-1 West Siding - Lower

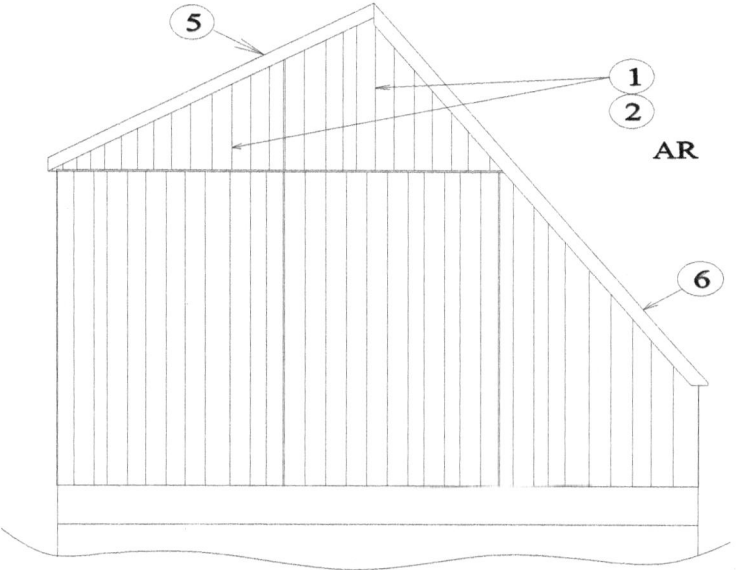

Figure 2.6-2 West Siding - Upper

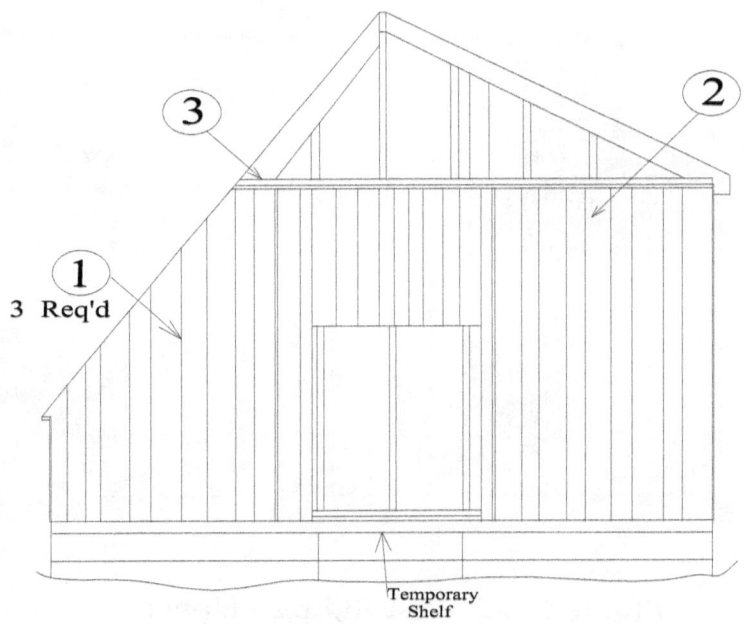

Figure 2.6-3 East Siding - Lower

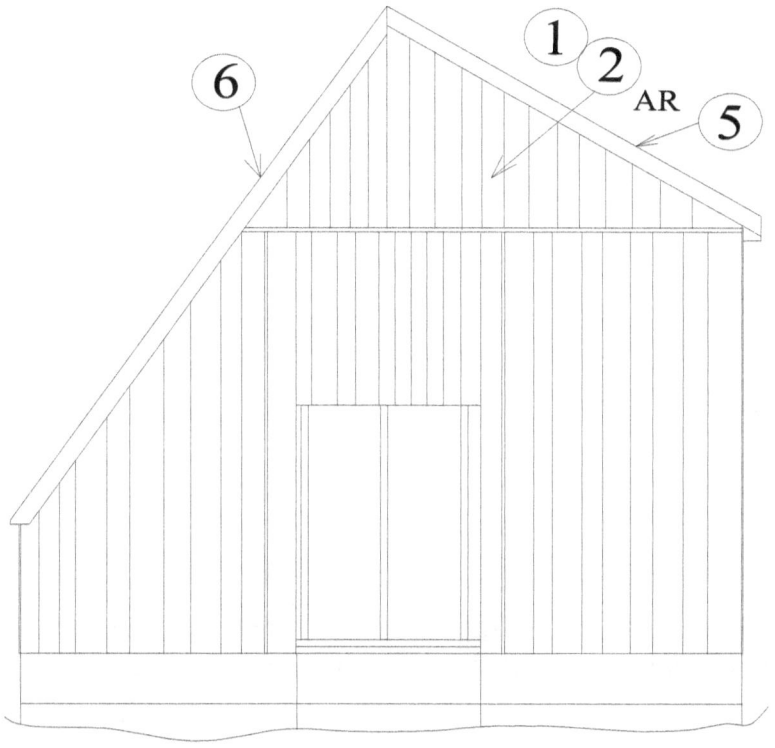

Figure 2.6-4 Siding East Side - Upper

Table 2.6 East and West Wall Siding Parts List

Item	Qty	Description	Source	SKU
1	12	Texture 1-11 Siding 4'x8' x .35"	Home Depot	509095
2	AR	Stainless Ribbed Nails 2" – 13 Ga	Lowes	41976
3	6	2"x0.63"x 120" Galv. Z Flashing	Lowes	366842
4	1	2"x4" 12' Board	Home Depot	161667
5	2	1" x4" x 8' Board	Home Depot	1001753944
6	2	1" x4" x12' Board	Home Depot	1001753958

2.7 Roofing

The roof sheathing is ½" plywood and is installed on the North Side rafters per Figure 2.7-1, while limited on the South Side rafters as shown in Figure 2.7-2. After the sheathing is in place, roll on the synthetic underlayment. This will protect the plywood and is the preferred underlayment for metal roofs. Then furring strips are screwed into place, which serve as a base for attaching the metal ribbed roofing. The roofing panels are fastened with special screws that have a rubber washer underneath and provide a weather seal.

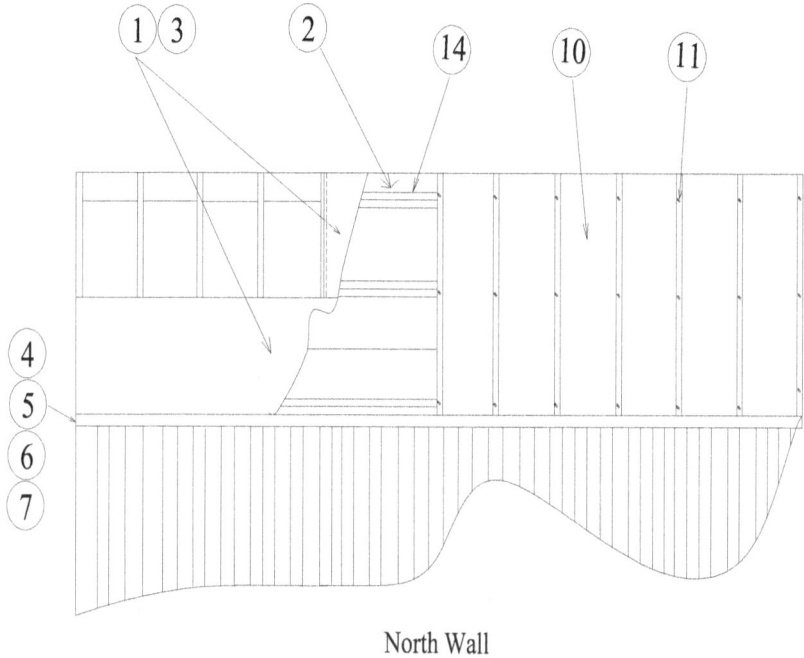

North Wall

Figure 2.7-1 Sheathing, Underlayment, Metal Roof

To allow as much sunlight as possible into the greenhouse, polycarbonate panels will be used on most of the south-facing rafters as well as the small south-facing knee wall. Provide for at least a 3-inch overhang at the bottom of the rafters. These polycarbonate panels are dual-layered, which provides better insulating properties than other plastic panels. They do not yellow, weather well, are durable and allow sunlight to penetrate very well. The metal roofing at the top should be cut long enough so that it overlaps onto the polycarbonate panels. Unique H-shaped polycarbonate channels are secured to the rafters at 4-foot intervals between the polycarbonate panels. Apply a bead of caulking/sealant to the H sections prior to inserting the panels. Once both sides are completely covered with the metal roofing, install the ridge cap.

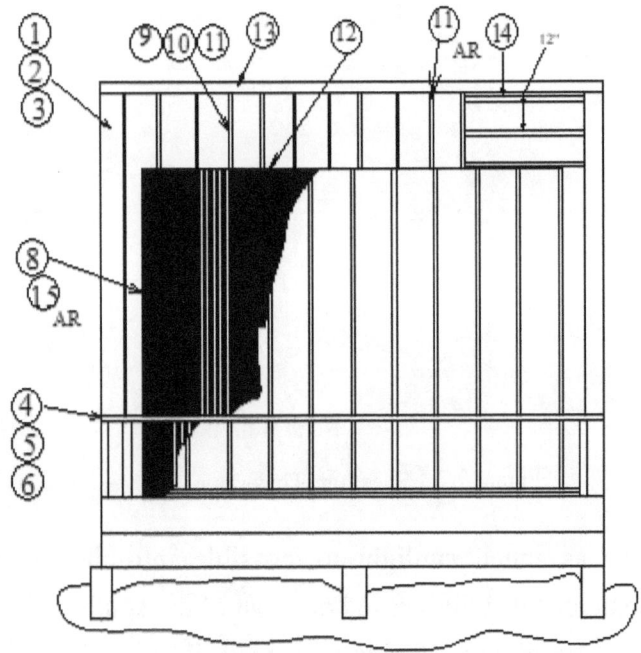

Figure 2.7-2 Sheathing, Underlayment, Metal Roof
(South Side)

Table 2.7 Roofing Parts List

Item	Qty	Description	Source	SKU
1	10	4' x 8' x 1/2" Plywood	Lowes	721366
2	5	Peel & Stick Roofing 3' x 50'	Home Depot	977115
3	AR	2" – 12 Ga Common Nails	Lowes	69120
4	2	1" x 4" x 12' Primed MDF	Lowes	229547
5	2	1" x 4" x 8' Primed MDF	Lowes	1291172
6	AR	Stainless Ribbed Nails 2" – 13 Ga	Lowes	41976
7	4	10ft – 29 Ga Drip Edge	Home Depot	1005774753
8	3	48" x 96" x ¼" Polycarbonate Panel	Home Depot	1003547497
9	2	Crimp Metal Roofing – 36" x 144" 29 Ga	Home Depot	1007322758
10	8	Crimp Metal Roofing – 36" x 96" 29 Ga	Home Depot	1007322702
11	AR	#9 x 1" Sharp Point Roofing Screws	Home Depot	183948
12	5	H-Section Channels 96" x ¼"	Home Depot	1000119357
13	4	Forest Green Ridge Cap – 48"	Home Depot	1000215958
14	AR	1" x 2" x 8' Press treated	Home Depot	315412

		Fur Strips		
15	AR	2 in. Screw for 5/8 in. Polycarb Sheet	Home Depot	1001753727

2.8 Insulation

To minimize heat losses, insulation will be applied between the rafters in the ceiling and between the studs on the walls. It is a rigid foam board type, called FOAMULAR, that has an R-10 insulating value. It is easy to cut into 14-1/2" widths and, resists mildew, and does not emit any hazardous fiberglass. To hold in place, use ¼" furring strips 1 foot in length and spaced every 2 feet.

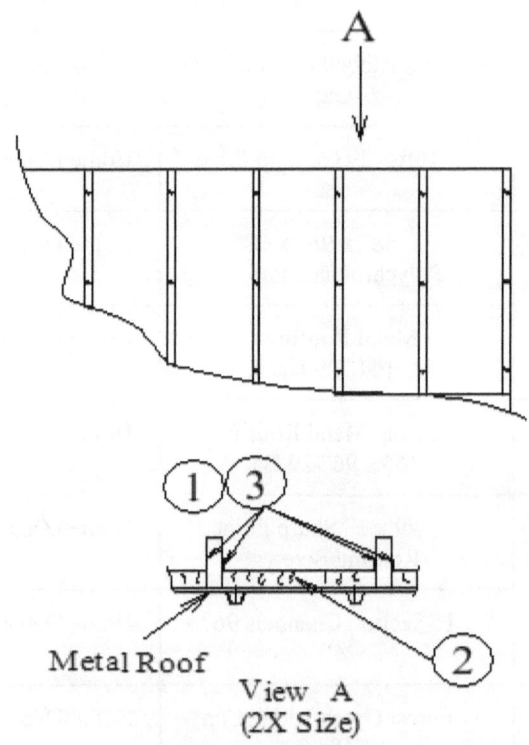

Figure 2.8-1 Interior Insulation

Table 2.8 Insulation and Paneling Parts List

Item	Qty	Description	Source	SKU
1	AR	Flat Hd Wood Screws #12 x 3/4"	Home Depot	284773
2	AR	FOAMULAR F-250 2 in. x 4 ft. x 8 ft.	Home Depot	1006240690
3	AR	Furring Strips 1/4" x 1- 1/ 2"	Home Depot	1001311054

2.9 Ventilator - Air Conditioner and Retractable Cover

For greenhouses that are not in the shade, a temperature-activated ventilator or air conditioner will be required. The best location is at the high end of the West wall. The dimension for the hole size is shown for both. By using a Dutch/split door at the entrance, the upper part of the door can be a framed screen that allows cool air while also preventing the entrance of insects, birds, and animals into the greenhouse.

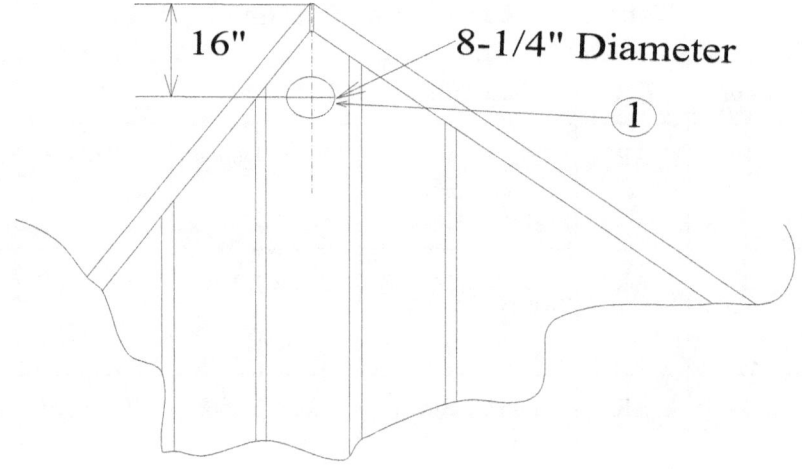

Interior View West Wall

Figure 2.9-1 Ventilator Installation

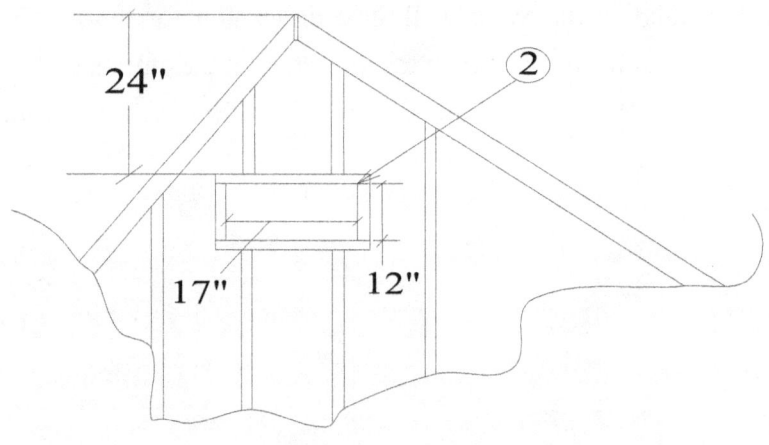

Interior View West Wall

Figure 2.9-2 Air Conditioner Installation

Retractable Cover

The Retractable Cover (See Figure 2.9-3) is used to prevent heat from being lost through the polycarbonate panel section of the south-facing roof during cold months. The retractable cover is a heavy-duty 12' x 16' tarp. For added protection, an optional thermal blanket of reflective insulation can be applied between two tarps using either zip-ties or duct tape. Three ropes are attached to the eyelets of the tarp, one at each end, while a third is in the middle of the tarp for both the North and South Sides of the roof. Screw Eyelets anchored into the South and North Base Walls are required for tightly securing the tarp to the surface of the polycarbonate panels. An informative App is available on the internet called SunEarthTools.com [10], which provides a customized angle and azimuth of the sun for your location for the entire year.

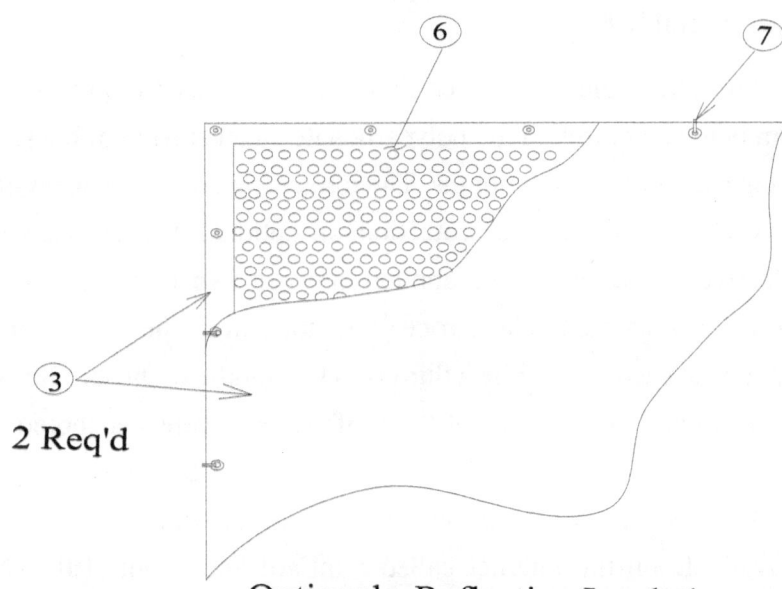

Optional - Reflective Insulation zip-tied between two tarps

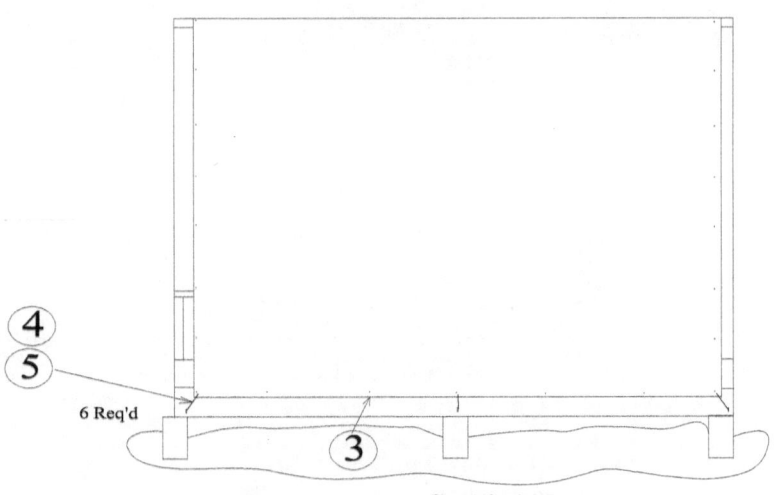

South Side

Figure 2.9-3 Retractable Cover Deployed

Table 2.9 Ventilator Air Conditioner and Retractable Cover Parts List

Item	Qty	Description	Source	SKU
1	1	Two-Speed Thru Wall Fan	Home Depot	1003574667
2	1	Air Conditioner 5,000 BTU	Home Depot	1005786787
3	2	Heavy Duty Tarp 12' x 16' x 5 mil	Home Depot	230641
4	3	Cord – 3/8" x 100 ft.	Home Depot	706036
5	6	1/4 " x 2-1/2 " SST Screw Eye	Home Depot	373748
6	2	SmartSHIELD -5mm 24" X50ft Reflective Insulation	Amazon	SmartSHIELD - 5
7	2	4" cable zip-ties	Home Depot	295780

2.10 Shelving

This greenhouse derives a good portion of its yield by utilizing vertical farming, so shelving is part of the design. Support columns are attached to the base walls and extend to a lateral plate that spans across the north-side roof rafters. They are an integral part of establishing vertical farming. Using a string attached to a plumb bob, position the bob over the outside surface and the East end of the garden bed. This will establish a reference line for the rafter where the lateral plate will be installed. Mark a vertical line where the string intersects with the rafter. Then drive a nail 2 inches below the reference line into the rafter. This will serve as the lower edge for the lateral plate. Repeat this procedure for the West side of the garden bed.

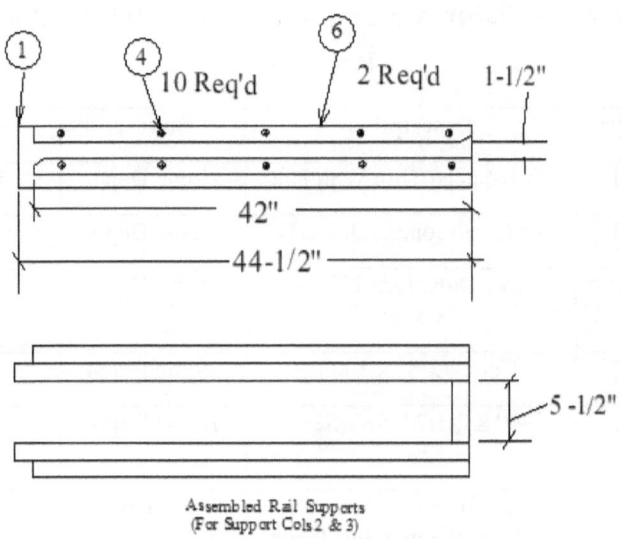

Figure 2.10-1 Horizontal Rail Support SubAssembly

The horizontal rail assembly consists of two shelf guides that are each 1-1/2" x 1-1/2" pressure-treated boards fastened to 2" x 6" boards to support the retractable shelves. These rail subassemblies are secured to the column supports and the rail support end plate along the North wall with angle brackets. They will be the main carrying members that hold up the retractable shelving. They must be square to the rail support end plate, while also being parallel to the opposite horizontal rail assembly.

See Figure 10.2-2 and Figure 10.2-3.

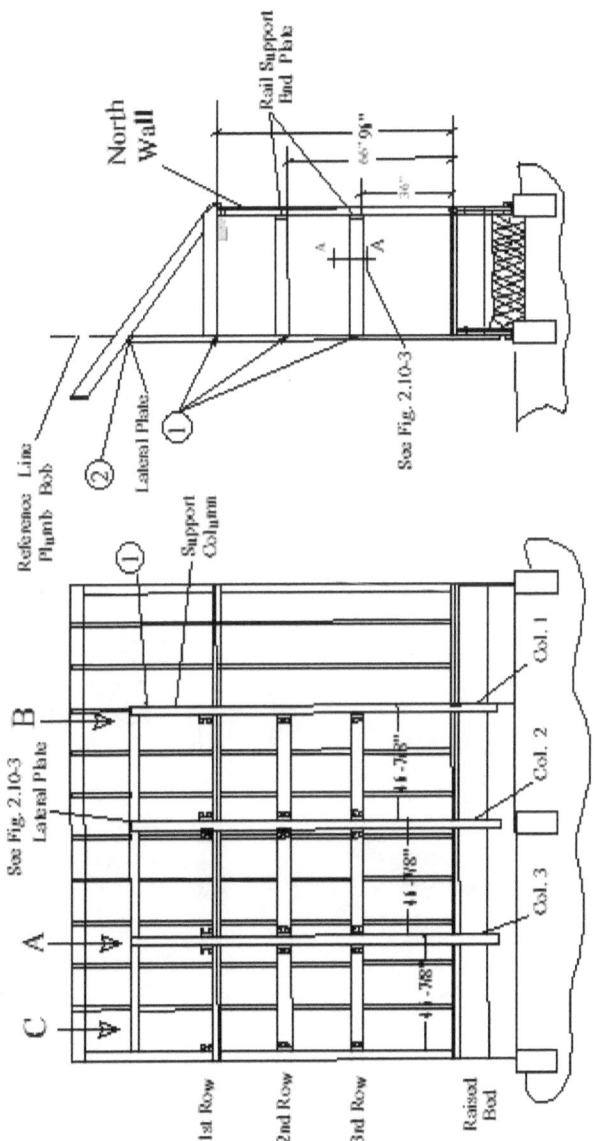

Figure 2.10-2 Column Support for Shelves

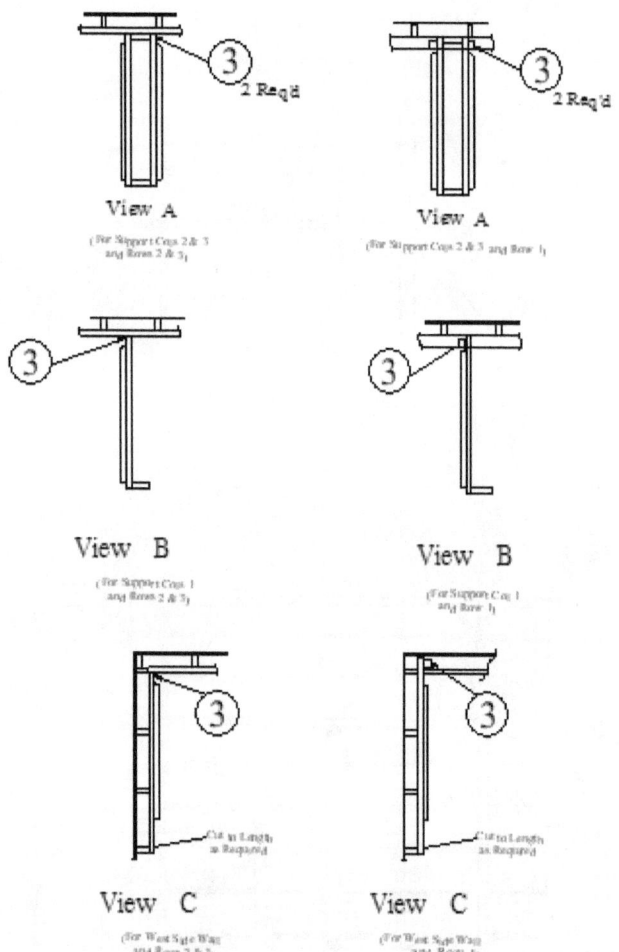

Figure 2.10-3 Column Support Details

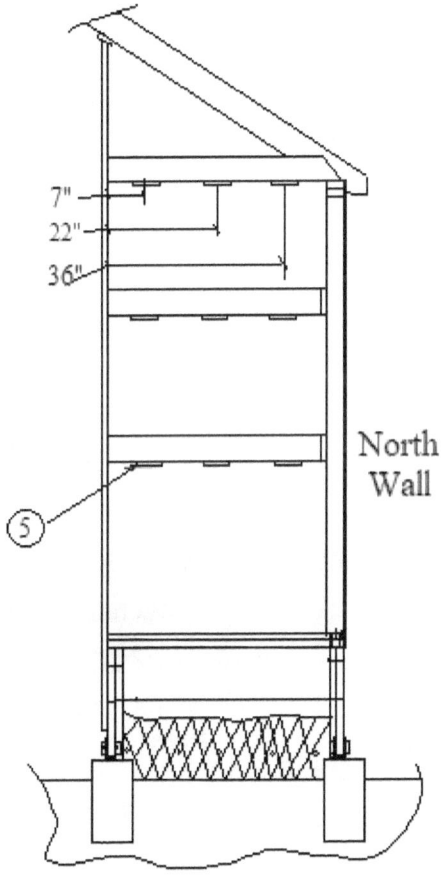

Figure 2.10-4 LED Support Boards

Table 2.10 Shelving Supports Parts List

Item	Qty	Description	Source	SKU
1	11	2" x 6" x 8' board	Home Depot	1001787120
2	4	2" x 4" x 12' board	Home Depot	603597
3	12	Alum Angle Bracket 2" x 4"	Home Depot	474657
4	AR	3" Squeek Screws	Home Depot	1000863053
5	9	1" x 6" x 12' board	Home Depot	914770
6	32	2" x 2" x 42" Press Treated	Home Depot	430400
7	1	Steel Plumb Bob	Home Depot	679259

2.11 Plumbing

The heated water is generated by a hot water tank and circulated by a water pump. Both are mounted on a sheet of plywood ¾" x 24" x 24" that is secured to the East Wall. An overall Plumbing Schematic is illustrated in Figure 2.11-1. Figure 2.11-2 provides a detailed view of what will be required to install the water tank and plumbing fittings to the circulating pump.

Water Tank

The water tank has a built-in thermostatic control dial for setting the temperature of the heated water. It has three ports: one for the inlet – with a blue ring, the outlet with a red ring, and an overheat/overflow port for safety reasons. The hot water inlet port and output ports require a female thread to the PEX tubing adapter. The venting port requires a male thread for PVC tube fitting. The inlet port to the water tank will take in the water that has been circulated through the raised beds. The output port is identified as blue. On the water tank, a PEX tubing line is routed from there to the inlet of the circulating pump. For the inlet port, a shutoff ball valve is located at the top so water and alcohol can be readily added to the plumbing as needed. Power outages are always a concern since this could result in freezing. To eliminate this possibility, mix a percentage of alcohol (high-proof bought at the local liquor store) with the water for use in the plumbing system. Using toxic car antifreeze poses a danger of plant contamination in the event of a leak. Pre-mix the alcohol with water in a one-gallon container before adding it to the water tank. A temperature coolant tester can be purchased at an auto supply store that can be used to determine the freezing point of the liquid mixture of alcohol and water. Alcohol should be evenly distributed in the water to obtain a good measurement of the freezing point of the water-alcohol solution. See Figure 2.11-2.

Water Pump

The water pump is located beside the water tank and is mounted to the same sheet of plywood. It has separate input and discharge flanges that allow for quick mechanical removal of the pump without cutting the existing plumbing lines. The water pump is controlled by a thermostatic relay, which will turn on the pump once the soil temperature falls below a certain set point. This water pump is sized to deliver adequate flow and pressure and draws very little current.

PEX Routing

The PEX tubing routed to and from the garden bed needs to be buried at least 6 inches and enclosed in insulated pipe wrap upon entering and leaving the garden bed.

NOTE

A temperature/ hydrometer probe for the soil is also recommended for monitoring soil temperature and moisture content. A Wi-Fi-enabled probe can be used for remote monitoring with a smartphone.

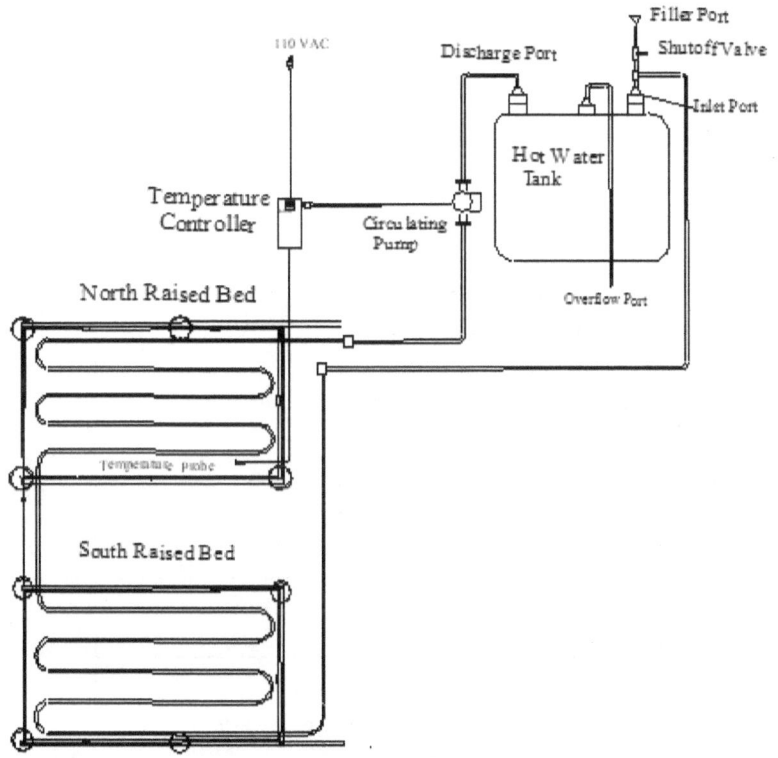

Figure 2.11-1 Plumbing Schematic

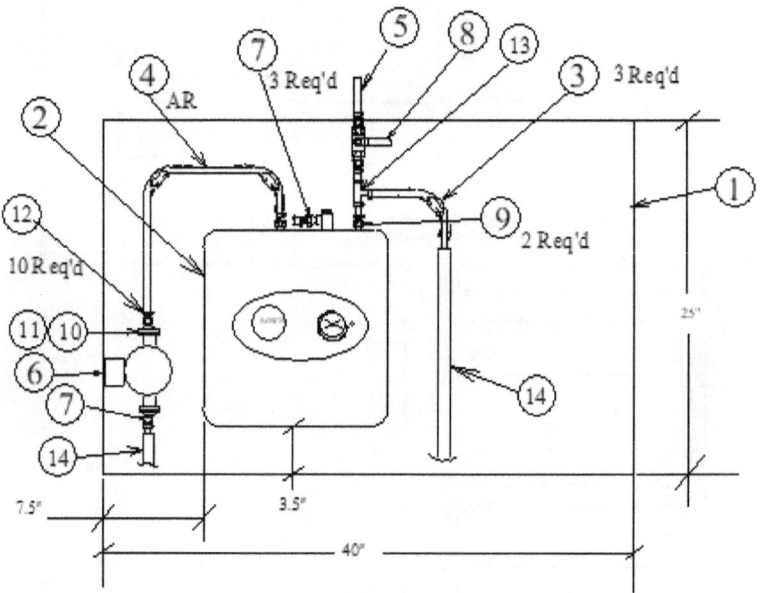

Figure 2.11-2 Water Tank/Circulating Pump Installation

Table 2.11 Plumbing Parts List

Item	Qty	Description	Source	SKU
1	1	Plywood – ¾" 24" x 48"	Home Depot	1826
2	2	Bosch 2.5 Gall Elec Tank	Home Depot	#ES 2.5
3	3	1/2 in. PEX 90-Deg Bracket	Home Depot	1002405003
4	AR	½" x 10' PEX Pipe	Home Depot	30-05010HD
5	1	1/2" Clear PVC x 18"	Amazon	B07TZ8X62S
6	1	Circulating Pump 1/25 HP	Home Depot	463132
7	2	3/4" NPT to 1/2" Barb	Home Depot	264403
8	1	1/2" FNPT Brass Ball Valve	Home Depot	107-403EB
9	2	1/2" FNPT to 1/2" Barb	Home Depot	264133
10	2	Red Rubber Flange Gasket	Home Depot	846333
11	2	Adapter Flange 3/4" FNPT	Home Depot	463140
12	10	SST Hose Clamp ½ to1-1/4"	Home Depot	602046
13	1	1/2 Barb Tee PEX	Home Depot	1003276346
14	6	¾" x 6' Foam Self-Seal Pipe Insul.	Home Depot	1000031794
15	1	Temp Stick Remote WiFi Temp & Humidity Sensor	Amazon	TEMP-STICK-THK-FBM

2.12 Wiring

The electrical sub-panel in the greenhouse should be rated at 60 amps. For some, the services of an electrician can best be served to make the proper connections. This chapter serves as a guide for what materials will be needed, as well as a detailed layout of the conduit and fittings required. This design also assumes there is an available source of electrical power via a main circuit breaker nearby. A power line will need to be routed and buried (18 inches) from the main breaker panel to the entrance of the greenhouse. Service to the greenhouse should be 55 amps minimum, so the recommended wire gauge is #6 in copper–UF (Underground Feeder type) for underground burial use.[9] The feeder wire connected to the sub panel will provide power to the hot water tank, circulating pump, LED lighting, overhead lighting, and ventilator fan. The duplex outlet power for the water tank and water pump shall contain a GFCI (Ground Fault Circuit Interrupter) approved, with a reset button built into the outlet.

Periodic testing of the GCI circuitry should be performed. The largest draw of current in the greenhouse will come from the LED lighting. This can be limited by applying power to the LEDs at different times via mechanical timers. The water tank draws approximately 12 amps and should only have power applied when it is full of water. Since the tank comes equipped with a cord and plug, its' receptacle will be mounted above the water tank. The water pump requires approximately $1/25^{th}$ of a horsepower and should draw less than 1 ampere to distribute water within the system. An optional feature would be the inclusion of a power monitor. This can provide a daily and weekly measurement. All the LED lighting is connected to one 30-ampere circuit breaker. In the interest of safety, the wiring from the electrical panel to the LED lighting is enclosed within a 3/4" electrical conduit. The main feeder line is along the ridge rafter and then separately branched out to separate mechanical timers that control the lights to the raised bed and rows 2 and 3. Each row has a distributed network of duplex outlets that are attached beneath the shelving horizontal rails.

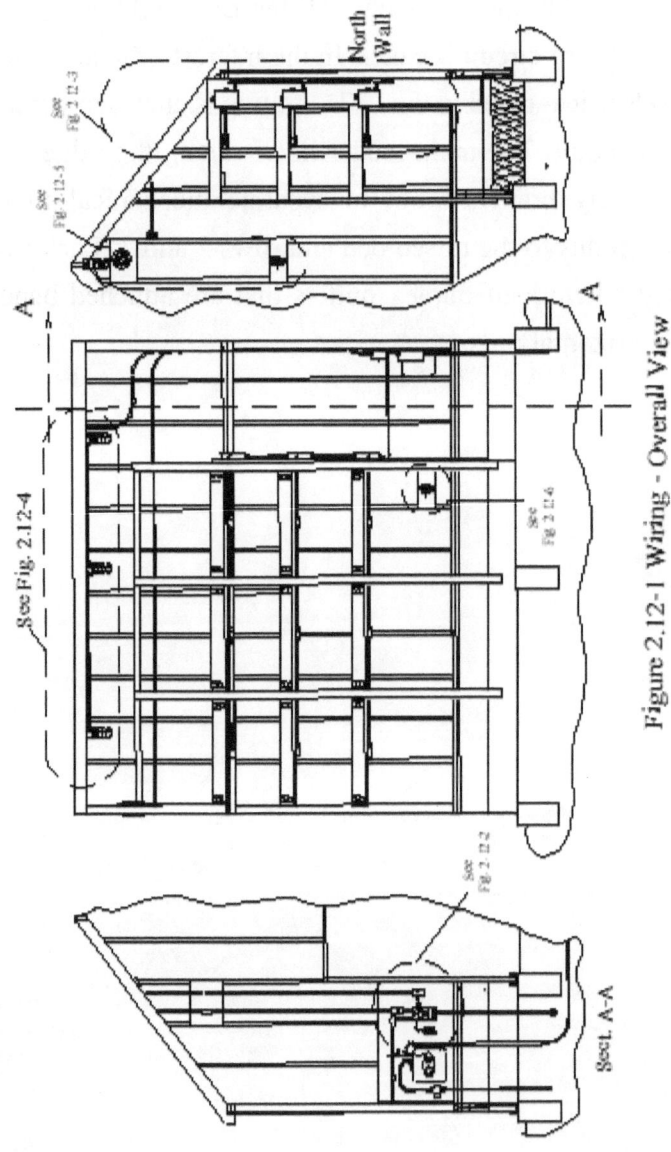

Figure 2.12-1 Wiring - Overall View

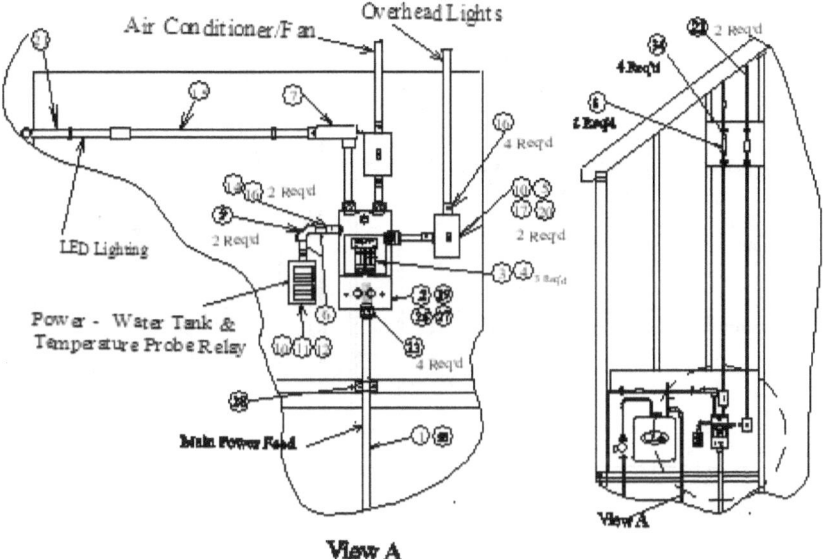

Fig. 2.12-2 Wiring - Main Panel Circuits

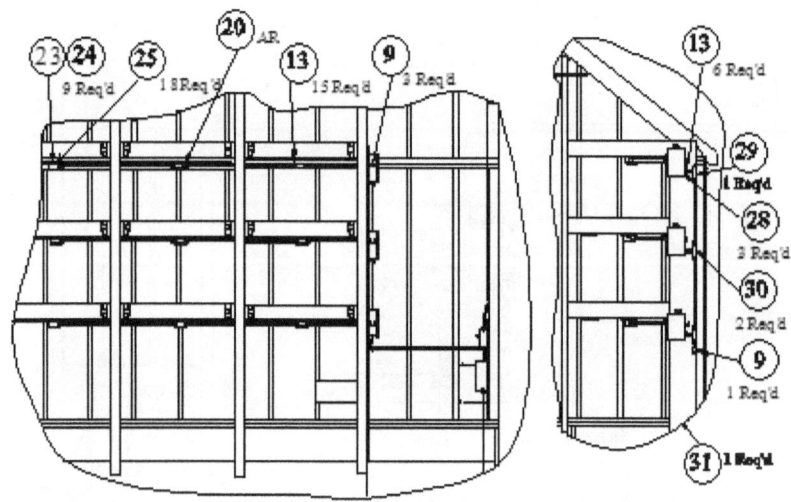

Figure 2.12-3 Wiring LEDs

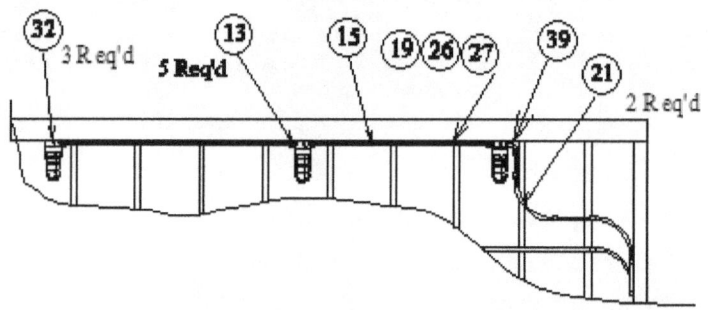

Figure 2.12-4 Wiring - Overhead Lighting

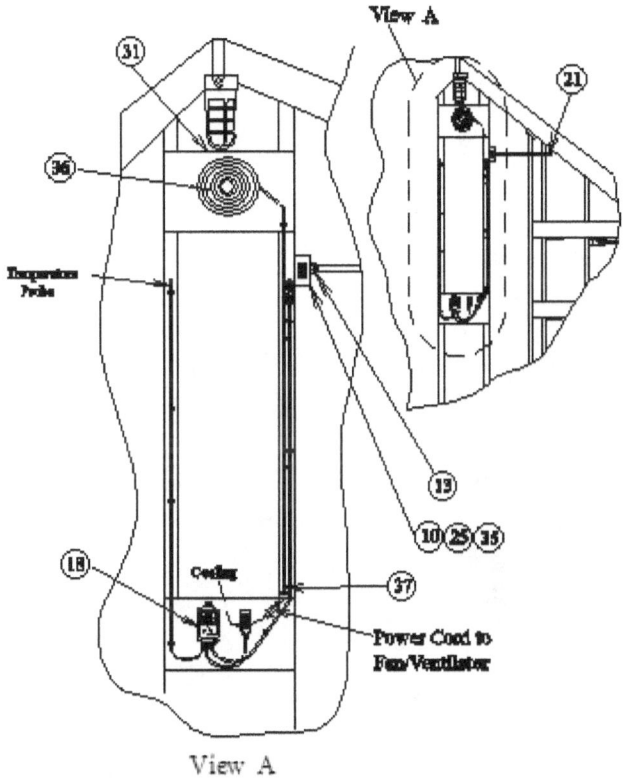

View A

Figure 2.12-5 Wiring - Thermal Switch
Air Conditioner/Ventilator

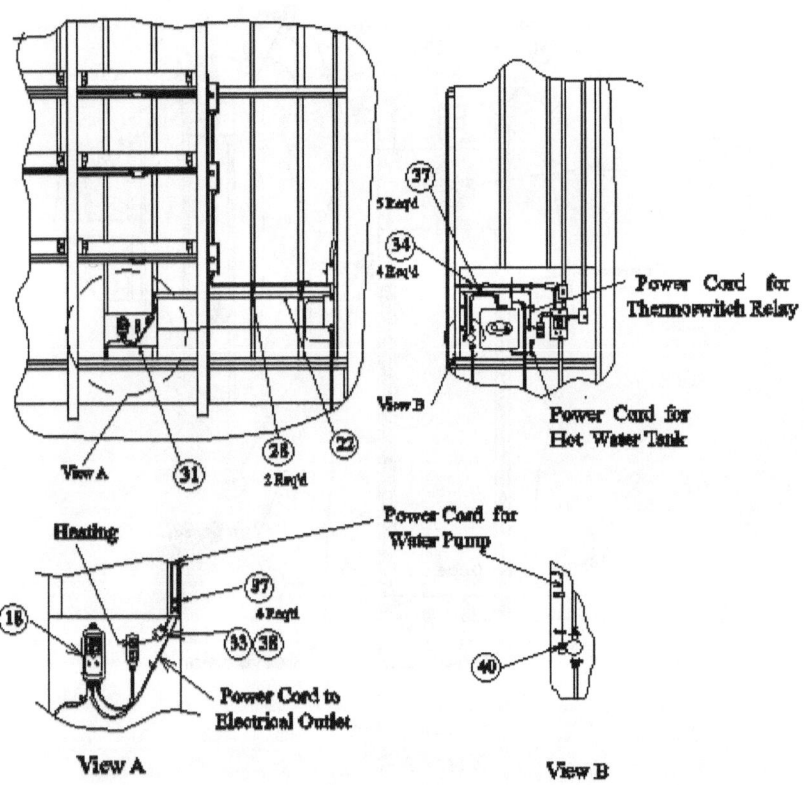

Figure 2.12-6 Wiring - Thermal Switch Raised Bed

Table 2.12 Wiring Parts List

Item	Qty	Description	Source	SKU
1	1	55 Amp - #6 – 2 Ga cable – 50 ft	Home Depot	28894422
2	1	60 Amp Panel 4 Circuit	Home Depot	E0204ML1060F
3	1	20 Amp Circ Breaker	Home Depot	576387
4	3	15 Amp Circ Breaker	Home Depot	576379
5	1	Electrical Switch Cover	Home Depot	58C30-25R
6	1	1/2" Metallic Electrical Conduit	Home Depot	0550005000
7	1	1/2" Sch 40 PVC – 90 Deg Conduit	Home Depot	E984D-CTN
8	2	1/2 in. Sch 40 PVC Type-C Conduit	Home Depot	E987D-CTN
9	1	1/2" Metallic 90 Pull Elbow	Home Depot	218286
10	2	RACO Std Electrical Box	Home Depot	70967
11	1	20 Amp Duplex GFCI Outlet	Home Depot	1001370813
12	1	Duplex Weatherproof Outlet Cover	Home Depot	WCDH1G
13	12	1/2 " PVC Conduit Fitting Conn.	Home Depot	1000032437
14	6	1/2 " Rigid Conduit Locknuts	Home Depot	26190
15	AR	1/2 in. PVC Conduit	Home Depot	67447
16	6	1/2 " Elect Tube (EMT) Conn.	Home Depot	26270

17	2	Electrical Switch 120v – 15 Amp	Home Depot	R52-01451-02W
18	2	Temper. Relay/Temper. Probe	Amazon	B011296704
19	1	Wire Green – Solid Copper 14 Ga	Home Depot	1000112518
20	AR	Red WING-NUT Wire Connectors	Home Depot	623622
21	4	1/2" Sch 40 PVC 90 Deg.	Home Depot	703266
22	1	2" PVC Conduit	Home Depot	184040
23	9	Metal 2- Gang 2 Device Wall Plate	Home Depot	1007804377
24	9	4" x 1-1/2" Square Box	Home Depot	1007804458
25	18	Duplex Outlet – 15 Amp	Home Depot	162677
26	2	Wire Black – Solid Copper 14 Ga	Home Depot	1002352610
27	2	Wire White – Solid Copper 14 Ga	Home Depot	713614
28	3	2" PVC Clamps	Home Depot	1004958664
29	1	1/2 in. LR Conduit Body (Elbow)	Home Depot	876964
30	2	1/2 " Sch40 PVC Type-T Cond	Home Depot	E983D-8-HD
31	1	1" x 12" x 8' Pine	Home Depot	458538
32	3	Hammered Black Light Fixture	Home Depot	1002711876
33	2	15 Amp 125 Volt 3-Wire Plug	Home Depot	1000050465
34	10	1/2 in. PVC Conduit Clamp	Home Depot	1004958678

35	2	Metallic 1-Gang Handy Box Cover	Home Depot	1000327675
36	1	Thru Wall 7-5/8 in. Transfer Fan	Home Depot	1003574639
37	20	1/4 " Plastic Cable Clamps	Home Depot	478468
38	1	14/3 Black Power SJEOOW Cord	Home Depot	1002352601
39	1	1/2 " 90 Deg. Plastic Right Angle	Home Depot	58133801
40	1	3/4 in. (NM) Clamp Connectors	Home Depot	279782

2.13 LED Lighting and Timers

LED lighting provides an enormous opportunity for promoting plant growth. It uses only 20% of the wattage consumed by traditional incandescent lamps for the equivalent output in lumens. [7]

This represents a dramatic cost savings. Since the 1st Row is meant for seedlings that have not sprouted yet, LED lighting is not required. As plant growth progresses, the individual seedlings are moved lower to rows 2,3 and eventually to the raised bed. The LED lights are attached to the 1" x 4" support boards.

The most beneficial LED lighting emits frequencies of red and blue. [8] Each plays a key role in having a productive garden. LEDs emitting a red frequency help the plant to flower and produce a higher yield, while the blue light enhances root growth, a greater number of flowers, and stronger stems. Connecting the LED lighting to timers additionally conserves electricity usage. Each timer controls the

ON/OFF times for the LEDs in that row. The selected unit is labeled as 2000 Watts but only draws 200 Watts. The Vegetative Coverage at 24 inches is 5 x 4 feet. And each row should draw about 6 amps when all 3 are turned on.

See Figure 2.13-1.

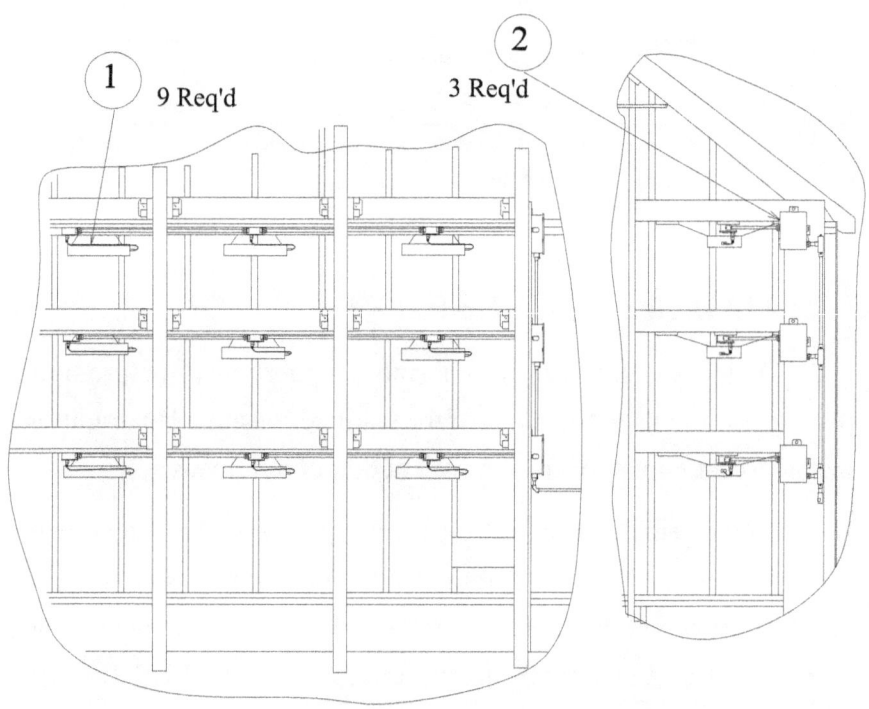

Figure 2.13-1 LED Installation

Table 2.13 LED Lighting and Timers Parts List

Item	Qty	Description	Source	SKU
1	9	P2000 LED Grow Light	Amazon	BESTVA 2000W
2	3	Mechanical Electrical Timer	Home Depot	46536

2.14 Shelf Design and Fabrication

As part of vertical farming, shelving will be incorporated to facilitate the watering and selective attention for the seedlings. Each shelve is a 38-3/8" x 48" box structure made up of 2" x 4" and topped with ½" sheet of plywood the same size. The shelve width allows approximately a ½" space on each side.

See Figure 2.14-1.

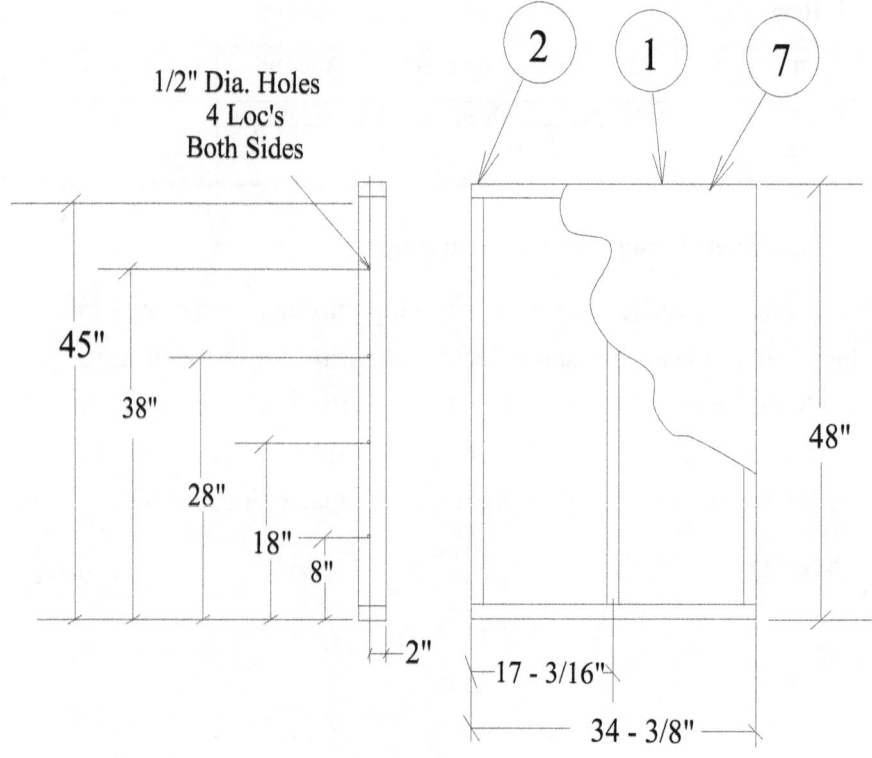

Figure 2.14-1 Shelf Design

Once fabricated, ½" holes are drilled in the locations as shown so they can accept bolts that are used to attach bearings on each side of this frame. As a subassembly, these shelves can be inserted between the horizontal rails and slide between the respective guides. Three washers are installed between the bearing and side rail to ensure the centering of the bearing over the horizontal guides.

See Figure 2.14-2.

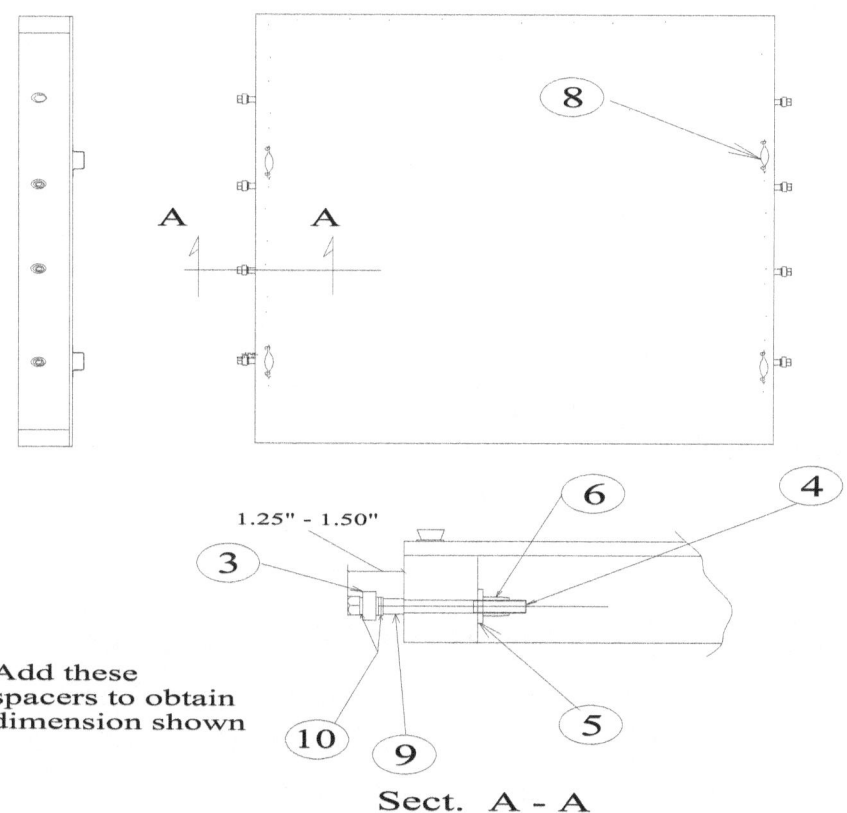

Sect. A - A

Figure 2.14-2 Shelf Bearing Installation

Table 2.14 Shelf Design and Fabrication Parts List

Item	Qty	Description	Source	SKU
1	2	2" x 4" x 12' Board	Home Depot	161667
2	1	48" x 96" x ½" Plywood	Home Depot	1001754124
3	8	½" Dia x 1-1/8" x 5/16" Roller Bearing	Amazon	R8-2RS
4	8	Hex Head Bolt Zinc plated ½" x 4"	Lowes	67374
5	8	Zinc Plated Washer ½"	Lowes	270067
6	8	Nylon Insert Hex Nut – ½" - 13	Lowes	180159
7	AR	Flat Hd Wood Screws #12 x 1-1/4"	Home Depot	251445
8	4	Drawer Pull - Colonial	Home Depot	1000669235
9	8	Nylon Spacer 1/2" x 5/8" x1/2"	Lowes	880445
10	8	Mach. Bushing 1/2 " x 7/8"	Lowes	882392

2.15 Preparation and Cleaning Counter

A separate space at the front left corner of the greenhouse is allocated to set up a counter in which to conduct both seedling preparation and vegetable clean-up after harvesting. The countertop is a pre-made butcher block type measuring 25" x 50" that can be further treated with a desirable stain or wood finish. A concrete block at the base of the outer 2" x 4" column is placed at ground level to prevent the counter from sinking.

See Figure 2.15-1.

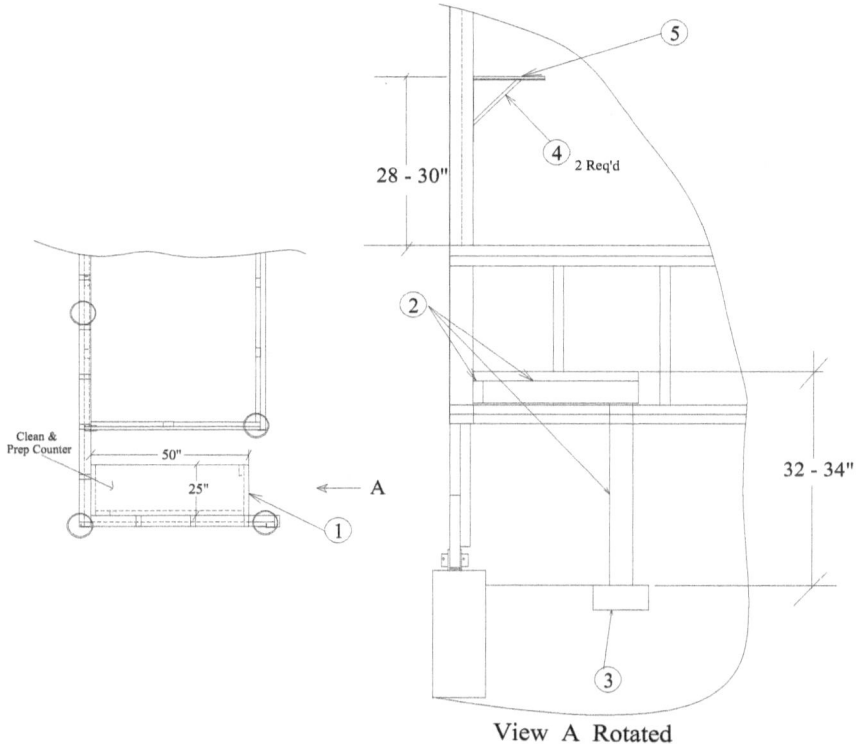

View A Rotated

Figure 2.15-1 Shelf - Preparartion and Cleaning

Table 2.15 Preparation and Cleaning Shelf Parts List

Item	Qty	Description	Source	SKU
1	1	Hevea Butcher Block Countertop	Home Depot	1007872021
2	1	2" x 4" x 8' Board	Home Depot	161640
3	1	Concrete Block 4" x8" x16"	Home Depot	559041
4	2	12" x 8" Heavy Duty Shelf Bracket	Home Depot	283726
5	AR	1" x 12" x 8' Pine	Home Depot	458538

Summary

The primary objective of this book is to reduce a locale's dependency on produce from distant farming locations. Most produce can be grown within this greenhouse. This design provides an opportunity for one to grow vegetables year-round that are free of pesticides and herbicides and minimize, in some cases, long trips to the supermarket. Recovering the cost of constructing this greenhouse can be hastened by selling the products to local stores and restaurants. Inflationary pressure on the price of fuel coupled with the indeterminant future of water being available for growers across the country will further contribute to rising food prices. This greenhouse is one way that individuals can make a change.

Bibliography

[1] Cash receipts by commodity State ranking (usda.gov)

https://data.ers.usda.gov/reports.aspx?ID=17844#P5713e5f0cac34ba5992e51b08aae31a9_2_251iT0R0x5

[2] Food-Miles and the Cost of Eating (stanford.edu)
http://large.stanford.edu/courses/2014/ph240/pope1/

[3] Agricultural Refrigerated Truck Quarterly Datasets | Agricultural Marketing Service (usda.gov)

https://www.ams.usda.gov/services/transportation-analysis/agricultural-refrigerated-truck-quarterly-datasets

[4] Vegetable Seed Germination Temperatures (harvesttotable.com)

[5] 2020 Electricity Rates By State (Updated Nov 2020) | Payless Power2020 Electricity Rates By State (Updated Nov 2020) | Payless Power

https://paylesspower.com/blog/electric-rates-by-state/

[6] Raised bed lumber, pressure treated safe? | OSU Extension Service (oregonstate.edu)

https://extension.oregonstate.edu/ask-expert/featured/raised-bed-lumber-pressure-treated-safe#:~:text=Of%20course,%20the%20primary%20concern%20with%20using%20pressure,arsenic%20in%20CCA-%20%20(chromated%20copper%20arsenate)%20treated%20wood

[7] https://learn.eartheasy.com/guides/led-light-bulbs-comparison-charts/

[8] Can You Use Any Blue and Red LED Lights to Grow Plants? (californialightworks.com)

https://news.californialightworks.com/can-you-use-any-blue-and-red-led-lights-to-grow-plants/

[9] Wire Size Chart (wiresizecalculator.net)

http://wiresizecalculator.net/wiresizechart.htm

[10] Solar Exposure

https://www.sunearthtools.com/dp/tools/pos_sun.php

Notes

www.ingramcontent.com/pod-product-compliance
Lightning Source LLC
Chambersburg PA
CBHW021835300426
44114CB00009BA/446